Feng Shui
Dynamics

The Door to Manifesting
Your Dreams and Decorating
your Home

EM "Penny" Crabtree

Feng Shui Dynamics

Published by Quality Life Publishers, 3594 Stockholm Rd., Suite 1A,Westerville, OH, 43081-4242

Printed in the United States of America

Library of Congress Cataloging-in-Publication Data
Crabtree,Penny
Feng shui dynamics; the door to manifesting your dreams and decorzting your home.
Volumn One The Feng Shui Course of Study
Library of Congress Catalog Number 2001116181

ISBN 0-9704556-0-7

Contents

Dedications   *v*
Using this Book   *vii*
Preface   *xi*
Introduction   *xv*

SECTION ONE

Chapter 1 The Truest Intention   3
Chapter 2 Understanding Our Reflection   29
Chapter 3 the Qualities of Life   39
Chapter 4 Our Bodies   55

SECTION TWO

Chapter 5 Reflecting Earth   63
Chapter 6 Designing Elements   75
Chapter 7 Decorating Elements   87
Chapter 8 Types of Chi Energy   97

SECTION THREE

Chapter 9 Qualities and the Bagua   107
Chapter 10 The Elements and the Bagua   119

SECTION FOUR

Chapter 11 Using the Bagua   131
Chapter 12 Adjusting the Bagua   143
Chapter 13 A Balancing Act   153
Chapter 14 Confirming Your Purpose   167

Personal Tutor Program   *175*
Contact information for workshops and classes   *179*
Professional Program   *181*

To Sandy and Sherry for believing in me.
For all the students that contributed; Betty, Josie, Kathy
and Christine who gave of her time unselfishly.
To my dear friend Yvette who taught me that
healing begins in the heart

Using This Book

Feng Shui

Feng Shui Dynamics is for anyone who wants to get the most out of Feng Shui with the least amount of time and effort. I think you'll find this first book in a series to be a straightforward, easy-to-read and an easy-to-use reference tool. With the premise that Feng Shui cannot effectively work for you unless you understand it, this book's purpose it to help you get a strong base in your understanding quickly and efficiently.

Let's face it — when there's a situation occurring in your life and you need support getting through it, or a goal that you want accomplished in record time, or when you are stuck in the middle and can't move ahead, there is nothing more frustrating. You want to know what to do — nothing more, nothing less — and you want to know it in a hurry!

That's what this series is all about. It's written in plain English — no technical jargon. Each section is broken down into only a few pages. That is so when you need to refer back for specific help with a problem, you can do so hassle free. This book is designed to give you practical applications so that you can apply them at once, incorporating them easily into your life.

While progressing through my own study of Feng Shui, there were a few things I was certain I wanted to know:

- As situations crop up in our life, how our surroundings support us.
- Knowing exactly how to make the changes ourselves.
- Learning at our own pace.
- And when questions arise, actually having someone to ask.

Feng Shui Dynamics gives you all that and more.

Three Great Ways

You are about to partake on what may be the most important journey in your life. I love Feng Shui; it is my passion. Not because it gives me all the answers to life's ups and downs, but it gave me the courage to try. *Feng Shui Dynamics,* is the easiest way to learn this art of purpose. You have three great ways to get the Feng Shui education you want in quick, easy manner that starts today.

Way Number 1 - Work at your pace

This book gently progresses though the work advancing your knowledge with each step. At the end of each section is an exercise. Completing these gives a more in-depth insight of how to apply these ageless principles to your situation.

The mechanics of this course are easy; the steps simple. The real challenge comes from within you. If you truly want to learn the mysteries of this ancient art, then spend time thinking about or meditating on, the exercises that precede the exercises.

Way Number 2 - Personal Tutor

With this book you have the option to register for your own personal tutor. Yes that's right! Upon registration, you will receive additional in-depth work sheets and a Professional Feng Shui Tutor to evaluate your work and offer advice when you need it.

Your Personal Tutor is here to answer *your* questions. If you need clarity on an assignment or if you have a question about your own home, your tutor is there to help.

Way Number 3 - Hands on classes

Workshops are being offered throughout the country. This course of study combines the work you do with that of other students taking the same class, so you can learn from a facilitator as well as from each other. These seminars are available for a more in-depth study of the material to further strengthen your knowledge of Feng Shui.

To learn more about any of these programs or to register for your Feng Shui Personal Tutor, see the back of this book.

Preface

A Personal Journey

Years ago I worked in a retail shop as a decorator. At times it was so hectic that I thought I wouldn't be able to make it through another day. I was very successful at my job, and reaped many rewards for that success except one - peace of mind. Back then, my husband and I had a saying about our jobs. We would say, "This is what I do, not what I am".

But that was wishful thinking and not completely truthful; we were our jobs. Our life was centered on what we did to make money. We planned our meals, our bedtime and even our yearly physicals around when we could get the time off. Every Sunday was a ritual of deep sadness to see the weekend draw to a close. Eventually, we found ourselves falling into a depression on Sunday evening because of the prospect of going to work the next day.

When I first found Feng Shui, and was able to apply it to my life, I did so with the noblest of motives: to bring the message of these wondrous life changes to others. What I didn't realize was that I had to live life first, and teach life second. In order to do this, the age-old question "What is the meaning of life?" crept up on me like a ton of bricks. If life isn't about survival, then what is it about?

Could it be that I had to leave the work - a - day world only to be come a servant to a deity that I wasn't sure I even believed in? No, the answer was that life is for *living:* work, repairs, family issues, etc., are supposed to evolve around us — not the other way around. The Dalai Lama put it so beautifully when he said, "I believe that the very purpose of our life is to seek happiness. Whether one believes in religion or not, we are all seeking something better in life. This will come about by training the mind; not in the cognitive ability but instead with a broader meaning of 'spirit'. With this, include your intellect and the *feelings in your heart* and mind."

There are many places we can go to feel most loved and wanted. Sedona, Arizona has earth energies that tremble under your feet. It is said the hand of God has touched Machu Picchu. Stonehenge, the Grand Canyon, Jerusalem, Redwood Forest, the Pacific Ocean, or your local park all have a life-giving chi residing in them. *Life giving* means to give life back, to nurture, to caress and help you feel terrific; to support your thoughts, your time, and yes, even your happiness.

It never ceases to amaze me that just when we think that we are at our lowest, the dynamics of life explodes. Something wondrous happens that gets us up and on our feet. It can be difficult to look at adversities and feel blessed; but they are blessings - carefully disguised — but blessings just the same. As a child I spent a lot of time discovering the world, and today I seem to be regressing back into that quite zone of exploration. This time the target is me. When I first started, the thought of getting "to know me" was scary because I didn't think I had much to like or even worse, I would have to go through a painful discovery process. Neither happened.

Actually, in the past few years I have made a conscious effort to understand myself better. To find what makes me feel really good and to avoid those situations that I don't like. In my search for ways to increase the quality of my life, I found an array of techniques and teachings that I never knew existed. Not only was I blind to these teachings, but also at first I was arrogant in thinking I could do just fine in life without them. There was the skepticism. I would ask myself, "What if there was a hidden agenda to these strange teachings?" That, of course, was my fear of the unknown.

Delving into areas that were foreign taught me that when we are open, the world not only gives us opportunities; it delivers them through an abundance of venues. Taoism, angels, the fairy realm, dowsing, reiki, macrobiotics, reflexology, Vasta, yoga, Christianity, acupuncture, meditation, aromatherapy, herbology, and hypno-therapy all have had a profound effect on my life - along with the masterful teachings of Feng Shui.

Perhaps a life-journey isn't a destination at all, but a secret location that we have deep inside the soul. A place where love and joy intermingle, and bliss is truly a condition of the heart. All we need to do is turn the handle and open the door.

May the Universe bless you as your journey continues.

Penny Crabtree
1999

Introduction

Universal Treasures

Feng Shui originated in China over 4000 years ago, and it has been practiced throughout the East in some form since that time. With the help of transportation, communication, and our willingness to discover new cultures, this Asian art was introduced in the West. It was first introduced over fifty years ago in the States but has taken time to mature to the public level. In the past ten years, the United States has exploded in its depth of teaching.

Within the past five years it has become highly accepted, and that was no easy task. Since our culture is based on a Native American foundation instead of Eastern teachings, Feng Shui had to be adapted to fit into our Western culture and thinking. In Feng Shui this feeling has turned into a science, a belief, a thought process, and to some - a spiritual evolution.

The feeling that "something" in the spaces where we spend time has an effect on your wellness is becoming widely accepted.

That "something" in Feng Shui is called chi. We Westerners call it energy, grace, life force, divine intervention, God, spirit, the universe, breath of life, life cycle, or spirituality - the list of names is endless. You can take Feng Shui to any level you wish. One thing is certain; lives change when you practice Feng Shui, most often quickly and quietly.

Flowing Chi

The underlying theory of Feng Shui is that everything in your surroundings - down to the smallest detail - can benefit or work against you, and chi energy is the force behind that change. If chi were left to always flow effortlessly throughout our lives, there would be nothing but good fortune. However, the items we surround our self with, the places where we spend time and yes, even our thinking, can alter that flow and at times bring it to an abrupt halt.

By understanding the current of this energy that flows through everything in the universe, you can arrange your home to keep the pathways as open as possible, and reap the rewards from an abundance of chi.

The initial source of chi is generated from the actual Universe.

The sun, stars and celestial bodies emit the chi that eventually filters down to our planet. It breaks down as it flows to our country, community, etc., until it reaches our front doors. It then disperses through our yards our homes, through each room, and around our furnishings until finally it reaches us.

As the chi energy moves through our homes, it produces certain forms and invisible patterns. These patterns then impact the shape of chi in our bodies. These patterns send out signals to the Universe and, like a magnet, draw life situations to it. Then, like a ripple in a pond, the chi is affected virtually all the way back to our country.

The closer the Universal chi gets to your personal chi, the stronger it becomes. Therefore, the chi in your home will affect you more profoundly than the chi that enters the country or community. Since chi energy draws abundance, you will want to insure that the abundance it is drawing is healthy and positive energy. By locating where the chi energy may get stuck, be too low, flow quickly or be to strong, you will detect problems before they occur, and be able to correct any imbalance by bringing the energy back into its natural flow. This order may be achieved by something as simple as moving your bed, changing your curtains, or painting your front door. Learning how to work with chi through the decor of your home can shape and alter many life situations.

Section I

Wisdoms

The Entry

Purpose:

Our homes play host to earth energies every day. Like an old friend, the entry of our homes should be warm, inviting and welcoming. When this is accomplished, the energies stay whole-some and enter in generous amounts.

Suggestions:

If the entry is dark use larger watt bulbs to lift it up. Have a "greeter" at the door such as a small tree in a pot next to the entrance or hang a wreath on the door.

Symbols:

Large house numbers and lighted driveways draw in the an abundance of chi as will: flags, wind chimes, whirligigs and fountains.

Color:

A red door will draw the chi of fast-action. Green doors symbolize growth. Black on an entry floor represents opportunity. Yellow flowers near the entrance symbolizes family unity.

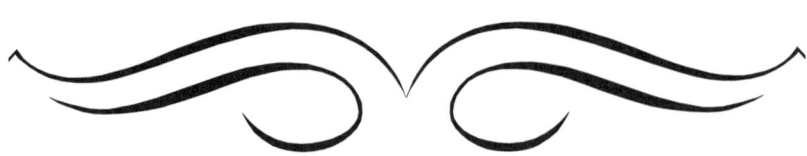

The Truest Intention

One morning I had decided to sleep in another fifteen minutes. Suddenly, I sat straight up in bed, realizing I had too much to do and believing that those fifteen minutes had just cost me dearly. The price was precious time that I did not have. As I ran down the hall to the bathroom, I stole a glimpse of the clock and came to a screeching halt. To my surprise I had not slept over fifteen minutes but had actually gotten up a half hour early. With my heart pounding as I tried to catch my breath, I sat down and shook my head.

"When did I allow life to do this to me?"

The *this* I am referring to is the rush to continue on with life while not paying any attention to what is best for me. Jumping out of bed in a state of panic and racing down the hall in a frenzy does no part of my body any good. My mind was disoriented and I actually believed I was late when in reality I was thirty minutes early. I could have stopped and looked over at the bedroom clock but I didn't. Why? My mind convinced me that I was already late. It shouted to me, "You have things that must get done today. You are an adult, people are counting on you, you're not allowed to indulge by sleeping in. Sleeping in is an irresponsible act."

The Root Of The Problem

Somewhere inside me a tape was playing these scolding words and I wasn't even aware as it happened. If I did sleep in, would fifteen minutes really be that devastating? Would my simple pleasure have caused harm? Rational thinking tells me no. My world does not evolve around fifteen minute intervals, and I doubt if yours does either. However, at that moment my thinking was anything but rational.

What had tricked my mind into believing that the opposite was true? My constant struggle with self worth. Feng Shui tells us that in order to fully understand the depths of its teachings, we must be able to connect mind, body, spirit, community and desire with self. In other words, we must come to a deep understanding about the connection of all things and their influence on us. The word us is the key here in understanding what we need to make us happy.

The first response to anything that made me take a look at myself was, "Ugh".

I would rather read ten books, write a thousand page essay or run a marathon than take a look at me. To me doing internal work or looking inside me meant that I had to uncover some nasty tidbit lurking there. Determine why I felt that way, work through the pain and then let it go.

I was wrong. Understanding what makes you happy through Feng Shui is simple. It is discovering what your deepest desire is, turning it into intent and acting upon it. It is not a painful struggle between self worth and value. It is a belief that all you desire is a gift: a gift from the spirit of the universe, given freely to everyone.

The Gift

I like holidays, my favorites are Christmas and birthdays. It's great to receive presents, especially when it's something that I have been wanting. Gifts from the universe are the same as any gift. We receive gifts from the universe every day but most of the time we pay little attention to them. Those gifts come to us in sweet water, clean air, food and clothing. These are the most precious gifts; the natural ones from Mother earth and the chi that surrounds them.

Feng Shui teaches that the universe is abundant in all things.

Abundance is apparent in the world itself. Have you ever tried to count the feathers on a bird, leaves on a tree or grains in one handful of sand? Of course not because we know that they would be infinite. So is the ability of the universe to give all gifts. The key is to tell the universe what it is that you desire. Not need, not want, but what it is that you truly desire.

That can be tough for those of us who struggle with self worth. Remember, this has nothing to do with anything you've done in the past. It's not a reward for accomplishments, but a gift of love. Internalizing is looking deep inside ourselves and to pinpoint the true desire. This desire is called intent. When we can verbalize, or put into words, our truest intent we are clearly defining what we need to nourish our soul and make us happy.

Simply Sara

Recently I asked a class I was teaching if the students knew their deepest desire. One woman spoke up and said, "My desire is easy, I want everything." I said, "OK let's take a look at that. Sara, between your job and volunteering you have little time to even plan your wedding. You and your fiancé have to steal moments just to chat. I would say you do have it all but with no time to enjoy it." "Perhaps, it would be best if you focused on just a couple things at a time." The student quickly agreed.

The word everything is a generic term for *all*. In the above case, that is just what Sara had, all the things she could handle. In protest we can guess that wasn't what she meant but from the above statement could you fulfill her deepest desire? No one could; not even the universe, because it wasn't clear what her desire was. Did she want more time, more money or a better job? Perhaps in Sara's case, it was to have more time to plan a beautiful wedding, but you wouldn't know that for sure unless she told you.

The universe is no different. By stating your true desire clearly and precisely there is no doubt what your intention is. When you voice your true thoughts and goals for all to hear, the message is intensive, clear and to the point. Stating true desire is an art that anyone can learn. It is quite simple -- putting dreams, thoughts and aspirations into verbal content.

Verbalizing our desires, or putting them into words, can be broken down in to a few short steps.

Find it -- the discovery process of the soul. Consider it-- narrowing our focus for the best result. Word it-- finding the words that convey how we truly feel. Affirming it -- knowing that we obtain it freely with no strings attached and then simply believing it.

Adventures of the Heart

Step One
Find It

 To focus on a desire let's begin by breaking up our life into nine areas: work, friends, children, relationships, reputation, riches, health, knowledge and self. In Feng Shui these areas are very similar to the ones we classify on a Bagua map. (More about that later.) Everything we do at every moment fits into one of these areas. These areas make it easier for us to focus on certain aspects of our life that carry individual importance. By taking a overall look at the way we feel about these areas our true desires begin to surface.

If we give something our attention resting our entire thought process on it and directing all our focus on it, we draw it to us. If we are putting our attention on the wrong things, they steal our energy leaving us drained and drawing unsavory experiences into our lives. Through our thoughts we give them power -- our power. When we focus our attention on the worst part of what is happening to us every day or the worst that could happen, in reality, we are drawing that experience to us. It is a simple rule, but one that is often ignored. To create your heart's desire, you must give it your full attention.

Restless Ruth

Ruth seemed to be plagued with more illness than anyone I knew. Every time we talked she was having another surgery or test. She had bladder infections, colon problems, back pain, high blood pressure and high cholesterol. Her life circled around doctors and medication. It was almost a "hobby" for her to visit a new doctor. No wonder her health never improved. By focusing her full attention on illness, rather then good health, she drew even more sickness to herself.

Once you focus your attention on what you want to create, you can then access your greatest strength, the power of intention. Life starts moving in the right direction when you put your attention on the true heart desire and then make it your goal to create it.

When you work with intention, set aside distraction, eliminate barriers, and constitute an association between yourself and your dreams. Intention begins to arrange your awareness so that you notice and seize upon all that you need to make your dream come true.

Clear directed thought
manifests clear intention

Intention is not like wishful thinking, which is abstract, unclear and submissive. Intention is like an arrow shot towards a target, it is directed and precise. Intention lays claim to your personal statement and creates the foundation of your dreams.

To find the intention, simply pay attention to what your heart desires. Notice I said *your* heart desires. Many times we focus our dreams on what others think we should have or what they believe is best for us. Even worse we take responsibility for the dreams of others neglecting our own. If you are living a dream that belongs to someone else, there will be no one there to say thank you when it's done.

As an interior decorator I worked in a wonderful situation. My schedule allowed me to work 9-5 most days. Being the coordinator gave me enough status to handle the large accounts, teach classes, and receive many promotions and awards. Other decorators were envious of my position calling it the perfect job, but I was miserable. It was the most sought after position in the company and I held on to it for nine years; though my real hearts desire was to work for myself. I was afraid, "What would people think if I just walked away." Eventually, situations happened that allowed me to leave to pursue my desire, and it began when I decided to focus my thinking towards moving on with the dream.

It's better to be honest and trust that people can adjust their needs if they must when you follow your heart. They may complain, but they can and will work things out. You will help people far more by being true to yourself and living your dream than by being angry, bitter and resentful. Often, the people we are putting ahead of ourselves are not even loved ones.

In my case it was a job, a collection of efforts that I got paid to do, it wasn't even a tangible person. We have been conditioned that putting others before ourselves, is a trait of a good person, but usually it isn't. It's an expression of fear.

Be open and receptive to all the Universe has for you.

For some of us it is traumatic just to make a change, or put in a little extra effort. We think that our desire is to mundane or not glamorous enough to be a true soul need. There is no such thing as a honorable or dishonorable desire. However, there are true *heartfelt desires* and then there are *should desires* that we adopt from others while trying to live up to a form of misguided loyalty. Find your true desire and keep it in front of you focusing on it with your full attention. Using the action of sheer delightful determination to achieve a wonderful result — your intention.

Exercises
Sit down and think about the things that stand between you and true happiness. Write them all down regardless of how trivial they seem. Perhaps it is something that frustrates you. Are you unhappy because you haven't had a raise in awhile? Is your love life at a stand still? Can you barely pay your bills each month? In the next week pay attention to anything that makes you unhappy and add it to the list.

Program students please complete Adventures of the Heart Work sheet Number 1101-1

Fine Tuning our Soul Choices

Step Two
Consider it

 Words are a funny thing. They take on different mean-
ings depending on the situation, sometimes just a
generation can change a meaning of a word. For
example what comes to your mind when you hear
the word "cool"? Cool can mean that something is
okay, or that an item is in style. The word cool can even mean the
temperature. One of the most unique ways to self-expression is
with words. Our words can have enough power to stay with us a
lifetime. They carry with them the responsibility of voicing a thought
and can even talk us out of a desire.

Most of us have little problem knowing what we want to say.
However, putting what we want to say into words can be challenging. Finding the right word or phrase makes most of us long for a
proofreader. When you begin by considering how things affect
you on a daily basis, describing them becomes easier. The philosophy that Feng Shui teaches is that by stating your desires, dreams
and wishes in clear terms you influence the outcome.

We are deeply affected by ordinary things. It is the simple
things in life we remember -- a pat on the back from your boss, the
way your mom added jelly to your peanut butter sandwich, and the
way it makes you feel to remember them. The way we feel about
things is what makes us unique.

We strive all our lives to be accepted as one of the gang — not
to stand out but to measure up to others thinking. The true fact is
that we are different; wonderfully solitary. So the way you feel
about life should come from your own perspective and always in
your own words.

Exercise
In ten words or less how would you describe yourself?

Program students please complete Fine Tuning Soul Choices Work sheet
Number 1101-2A

When I first did this exercise on my family and myself I got a combination of words like: love, joy, peace, family, giggle, rugged, spitfire and life. Every member of my family had a different list of words. The words had similar meanings but were personal to them. The amazing part about this little exercise is that, if you followed the directions, these words came to you with out much thought.

Words from a Higher Source

What if you had one chance to say a word that would change your life, a word so profound that all barriers melted away by simply stating a fact? Your heart would sing and you would become crystal clear in your thinking.

Could you do that without much thought? Most of us would require a quiet time to really think about what we wanted to say; to contemplate on how we stated our thought. Our attention would be focused on how to say what we dream so passionately on. How would our words change if contemplation and deep consideration would have been given to them?

Let's try the above exercise again. This time think about how the words make you feel. Consider how they affect you. Contemplate on their personal meaning to you. Take your time, all day if you like. Make them private, compassionate and full of conviction.

When you are finished review them. Is that really the way you see yourself on a daily basis, or is it what you are striving to become? Know that if this is what you are working towards, and then it will be so!

Exercise
Think about how you would describe yourself -- use the same heartfelt emotions you would in describing your very best friend.

Program students please complete Fine Tuning Soul Choices Work sheet Number 1101-2B

Consider it, Imagine the possibilities

If you can't find your heart's desire, maybe it's because you can't find yourself. Consider the possibility that you are so busy with life that it clouds your ability to perceive your needs. Our mind is a fascinating place, full of wonder and mystery. It is the basis of all our beliefs. As an adult, I had always been intimidated by escalators, choosing the elevator over them every chance I got.

One afternoon, my sister and I were at the airport to catch a plane. The quickest way to the departure gate was down the escalator. When I stopped at the edge of the step my sister turned to me and said, "Oh, don't worry about it, you won't get your foot caught, like Mom use to tell us". I was stunned; I had never realized that my fear stemmed from my mother's apprehension. Nothing traumatic had every happen to me in relationship to escalators, but all those years I projected a fear that wasn't even mine.

One of our natural gifts is to be able to handle our fear through love. But handling a fear that isn't even ours is impossible to walk through.

Your beliefs produce the history of your experience by etching the subconscious mind with orders. Each belief you accept is embraced by the subconscious mind as an instruction, which it then sets about following. The subconscious doesn't argue, it is very willing to give you back what you ask.

Your subconscious mind produces best what you dwell on. The more precise the thinking, the better the result. You've heard the old saying, "be careful what you ask for, you might just get it." Thoughts are very powerful anything that the mind thinks it can manifest. If you want love in your life then dwell on wonderful examples of love. If you want prosperity, focus on being prosperous. Focus your attention on these ideas until you believe them to be true.

The mind is powerful and will deliver anything you can think of. It is the place where your desires are nurtured and protected; where they are kept safe while they grow and develop. Your imagination feeds your dream, showing your conscious mind how it will take place. When the dream is ready for reality and can no longer be contained, your mind begins to deliver your dream through a birthing process.

Then get out of your own way. Drop any negative thinking that blocks you from letting the detail of your dream become clear.

Dream clearly and precisely

Feng Shui teaches that a desire is as pure as our heart. When you deeply consider your desire, you will be amazed as to how quickly it will materialize. You can tell whether something is a true desire or not by how well you can picture it.

Can you envision your dream? Can you touch it? What does it look, sound and smell like? Let's try a little experiment.

Close your eyes. Think about your desire. Think about a day when you will be living your dream. Where are you? Describe what that day looks like. See yourself in the middle of the picture. What are you wearing? What are you doing? Listen, do you hear anything? What is causing the sound? Is the picture in color? Keep focusing on it until it becomes a crystal clear image. When the picture is clear take hold the picture and draw it to you until it is right before your eyes. Study it well, find tune the details until they are sharp. Now, tell your subconscious mind, "This is my special desire, take it to the Universe and fulfill my dream. Thank you for all the support and love you give to me."

The Universe will listen to your desire, because it has to. It doesn't know not to. The subconscious has to deliver because it is a "yes man" which is doubling as delivery boy. However, you must do your part, keeping that picture alive.

Look at it in your minds eye daily. Surround yourself with symbols in the form of artwork, or affirmations and other constant reminders. Make a list of things that you need to have when you attain your goal. Keep it with you always. Do every thing you can to be ready for your goal. Feng Shui teaches us that with every change our life changes. Be prepared to make the necessary adjustments in your life, and when you're ready, go for it.

Exercise:
Make a list of things you need to have ready when your dream arrives. What symbol would be a constant reminder of your goal.

Program students please complete Fine Tuning Soul Choices Work sheet Number 1101-2C

The Gift of Speech

Step Three
Word it

 The Chinese believe that in order to optimize our lives to benefit us, we should consider the affect of everything around us. By considering how things influence us, we can make healthy decisions concerning what we will allow around us. Certain things can cloud our thinking, and when that happens, we lose focus on what is important to us. If focus is lost, we lose contact with our inner self. Each day there are things that can cause bumps in our peace and serenity. That is why it is so important to put our desires into words: words on paper. There is nothing better then to reread words that have been written in journal form.

Recently I was cleaning out a drawer and came across my daughter's baby book. I sat for a long time skimming pages and reading the words connecting me, once again, to this toddler.

Even though the words had been written twenty-five years before, those moments were as clear as if I were there again. The pages were not eloquently written. Some pages had just little scribbles in the corners, but what an insightful work of art it is. Words jumped off the pages like first, smile, tooth and laughter. Simple words remembered my daughter's youth.

Words and wordings are not the same thing. In the baby book single words were used to describe daily events as: first tooth. But wording our desire, describes how we long for a situation to turn out. Every time we sit down to write, we can create a beautiful passage between ourselves and others.

After you consider what your dream looks like, sounds like and feels like; you draw it to you. Putting into words what you see becomes an integral part of your soul searching. We connect to the universe on a higher level through the words used to describe our deepest desire. The right words convey that emotion, bringing our picture to life, making the desire real and tangible.

In my daughter's baby book the two words, first tooth, give us a precise point of focus. The event of a baby teething brings to mind a picture of a white sparkling gem in the mouth of a child. Lets say the baby book had simply said first year. Then the picture is vague. It could include many pictures, and there is some confusion as to which event to focus on.

Making specific choices aids in expressing our intent. Choosing simple words can add immense clarity in describing what's in your soul. Petite ballerina conveys a more crystal-clear picture than tiny dancer. Not only is the picture clearer, the emotion attached to the word produces a concentrated form of chi, one that is soul-drenched.

Look at the list of words below and on the next page. See if you can *feel* the difference between the words in the first column from the ones in the second column.

good	*wholesome*
fit	*healthy*
hot	*fiery*
cold	*frigid*
long	*extended*
hug	*embrace*
family	*ancestry*
picture	*image*

It isn't important that you be an eloquent speaker or have an immense vocabulary. Choosing words that are personal to you, however **is** important. Taking text and turning them into power statements is the first step towards the direction of fulfilling the dream.

Once you have the emotional feeling attached to your dream, make all the words that relate to it positive. When words are positive;

they are enchanting, like a beautiful song. The statement, I want a new job, has a wonderful ring to it when we say, I have a wonderful new job in management that I love. I am tired of spending my life alone, transforms when we state, I share my life with a wonderful, loving man.

Feel the difference in the following statements:

My son drives me crazy -- his life has no direction.
I have a wonderful, creative and enterprising son.

Every fall I get a cold.
Good health is a great part of my life.

I would like to have a good friend to talk to.
My life is full of friends that love and support me in all that I do.

Perhaps your desire is to have a great adventure that provides an income in which to live. That is a much better approach then to say "My job stinks, I am out of here." When we take away the mystery of the unknown by stating exactly what it is that we desire we put our self back into the equation -- right where we belong.

In Feng Shui "putting yourself back into the equation" translates into a better quality of life.

The concept of stating a deep desire can be challenging for some. We've been brought up to believe that desires, longings and passion are a form of self-indulgence; an indulgence that is thought to be selfish and self-centered.

Desires, longings and passions *are* a form of self-indulgence, but that is a good thing. Thinking about self is healthy, not a negative act. Doing things that fill our deepest needs, helps us to be more effective in helping others. How can you teach a starving man to read when all he knows is that he is hungry? You must feed him first, then he will be more able to learn what you put in front of him. The need here is to take care of self first. Regardless of how noble the act, others are served best only after we are fulfilled and content.

To sacrifice ones self is a form of self-abuse, and puts a negative twist on other things in our life. By keeping a clear picture and describing it in the positive, we bring the power of the Universe to our family, our children and to people we know. One thing is for sure, when your dream becomes a reality everyone will ask you how you did it.

Reinforcing Our Feelings

Through the art of Feng Shui we learn that what you feel has great influence on the vital chi in our homes. Saying what we feel in a positive and confirming fashion reinforces our feelings, magnifying the amount of chi energy present. This brings your dreams and desires into clear view.

Desire is not a silly whim. It is a deep longing that we desperately need to become whole. It is the anticipation of great things, but with no expectation as to how it will arrive. Rarely is life one extreme or the other though at times it can feel very extreme. Days can be really bad or really good, but generally it is some ongoing event that makes us feel that our entire foundation is tumbling down. These moments of living have such an impact that they stifle the mind, cause health problems and can overpower our entire thought process.

Certain things can happen
where we question our existence or, at the very least,
we lose the confidence to move ahead.

When we start to excavate our life, we find that there are maybe one or two areas that need taken care. But it can be tough to pinpoint these things when your whole life feels threatened. The question becomes, "How do I take care of those things positively when I can barely keep my head up?" The answer is, "You don't!" You begin to lay out your desire in clear steps so that the universe and spirit understands them. If life has been getting you down; then you wash your face, throw your shoulders back and ask for your heart-needs by wording in the positive.

The secret in verbalizing our desires, is to identify those obstacles and things that keep us away from our goal by stifling the energy that flows there, keeping us at arms-length. Energy can take on a new positive simply by rewording the way we address it.

To continue towards your dream, remove everything that takes your focus away from your desire. Look at all sides if it, consider any waste, clutter, distraction, or negative thinking. It means finding the time and the discipline to establish the proper habitat that your dream requires to grow. Then giving it all the nourishment it needs to do just that!

Exercise:
List one desire or dream that you have not been able to fulfill. Now describe it in detail. What does it look and feel like? Picture yourself in the center of the desire. What are you wearing? What are you doing?

Program students please complete: the Gift of Speech Work sheet Number 1101-3

Tip

Sleep with your bed against a wall; it will help you remember your dreams.

A Gift to Ourselves

Step Four
Affirm it

 The definition of affirm: a verb, to put firmly and with conviction. I couldn't have said it better myself. The most important part of this definition is that affirm is a verb. A verb is an action word. So when you affirm your desire with the truest intent, you are in reality confirming your convictions. What a powerful statement.

Feng Shui teaches us that in order to balance and organize your thoughts you must do so with the purest intent. This intent is the thrust, or the heart of your desire and spreads out around you. It is virtually impossible to have positive chi energy surround you and that energy not affect others. Healthy chi energy is so strong that simple affirming words layered with a pure intent will cause miracles to happen.

Where affirm is the act, affirmation is the confirmation that what you desire you also deserve. So how does one go about affirming a desire? Once you believe that you have found your desire and the words to write it down so that it is clear and precise, begin to find wonderful approving ways to take all negative energy away from it.

For example perhaps you always wanted to be in the theater. You decide that you want to join a local theater group. You're scared; fear is telling you that you have no talent. Maybe it isn't fear; maybe it's that sweet little voice inside your head. You know the one. It says things like, "Oh, now don't be foolish. You have no working knowledge of the theater. You just stay away and maybe we will go see a movie instead." Sound familiar? It is that sweet little voice that keeps most of us from trying something new. Actually it isn't even sweet - it's the voice of intimidation. A wolf in sheep's clothing and it has squashed more dreams than time, money or even age.

Love vs Fear

There are two motivations in life, love and fear. That is why you should begin to surround yourself by things in your home that are loved. When you do this your home becomes one big loving affirmation that keeps you uplifted and happy. When you are motivated by love, the efforts come easily. When the motivation is fear efforts are difficult and ineffective. You always have choices and they may require discipline but don't confuse discipline with punishment. Teaching yourself to make positive choices is much easier when your thinking is affirming. No real joy ever stays around for long when you are motivated by fear. Embracing your dream with positive enthusiasm is a form of self-love. Self-love takes a little practice but it is the most rewarding affirmation I know.

If being part of the theater is your dream, then state it; " I am going to be on stage in the theater." Then affirm it. "I have a wonderful part in a great theater group." Period! Then go talk to your local theater group. WOW, how simple and how exciting.

That's it, no red flags, no banners or marching bands. Then the universe is very clear on exactly what your heart needs. Your desire is stated as fact! To affirm your desire take possession of it. Claim it as yours. You have nothing to lose.

Peppy Pam

Pam had wanted to be an Interior Decorator all her life, but money and bad timing had prevented her from going to school and getting the necessary credentials. Now since her children were grown, she had many regrets that she hadn't followed her dream. In a conversation over lunch I told her that pursuing her dream was imperative for the soul to grow. Besides I added, "You are astonishingly talented." A short time later I received a call from Pam she had gotten a job at a decorating firm as a Creative Consultant, helping customers choose accessories for their home. When I asked her how she got the position. Pam answered, "I called every place that sold decorative supplies and told them that I was astonishingly talented."

Even before I started to practice Feng Shui I knew the power of our intention, the power of our deepest thoughts. But I never knew the magnitude in which thoughts can come into reality until I understood the limitless connection of our words to the universal chi energies that surround them. The fact is without Feng Shui, the reflection of your surroundings is much harder to keep in focus, harder to see the endless possibilities.

Affirming desires are never limited. You can have an infinite number of heart-needs. Some desires take a lifetime to fulfill, much like the work of Mother Theresa. Others take less time like finding the right college to attend. Nothing is to trivial, dreams don't have to be grand or exotic, sometimes the simplest are the best. However, all types of desires have a common factor —they are personal to you.

By using affirming statements you stop any negativity from creeping in around your intent. This shift in thinking, taking control of life, allows hearts to soar. Keeping the conscious mind in a positive motion does this. Affirming statements are approving words, and they have power over thoughts. They are the deepest connection between thought and self. They give you empowerment over your choices; your life. This feeling Feng Shui teaches, is a shift from positive energy to precise, expressive chi energy that is effortless and effective.

Feel the power in the below affirming statements.

I am prosperous in every way.
I am willing to accept my family.
Today is my wonderful day.
All my relationships are wonderful and loving.
I have the greatest trust in a higher power.
I am totally healthy.
I am filled with love and affection
I choose to make it so.

The two most powerful words in our language are " I am". When you say "I am", you add power and punch to your words and you can be certain that what you claim will come to be. The words "I am" denote ownership and are the most powerful words in the Universe. Knowing this can release all of your potential and manifest it into material form.

Whatever your dream is pretend as if you already own it. Fake it till you make it. If you can imagine it, it can come true. That which you think, you create.

Claim out loud who you are.

I am an actress
I am beautiful
I am a fire fighter
I am a playwright
I am priceless, just as I am.

Remember your Divine truth; open your heart and release, for all the world to hear.

The Universe will never let you be anything less than the god, and goddess that you are, and it completely respects your right to be so. Words spoken with conviction form chi magnets and attract back to the speaker exactly what was broadcast into the world. When words are spoken with conviction and confidence, they amplify the force of the Universe and deliver it a hundred fold. Conviction pulls your desires into your soul. Confidence guides them directly to you. Ownership, through your words, delivers them to your feet. With the Universe and spirit on your side, how can you fail? After all what's not to like?

Exercise:
Pick one of the obstacles that you listed in exercise one that blocks you from happiness.
Now reword it to make a positive, affirming statement. Let say you want to move, you
could say "I am moving into a wonderful new apartment, one that I love".

Program students please complete A Gift to Ourselves Work sheet
Number 1101-4

Knowing the Truth

Step five
Believe it

 As children we are taught many things, some of
which make us smile at how gullible we were when
we were small. The concept of Santa Clause, the
tooth fairy and the Easter bunny seem silly, but
charming, so much so that in many homes they have
become tradition. We are also taught other things as children that
are not as amusing.

Some ideas and certain forms of thinking are handed down
from generation to generation. Sometimes it's the very belief system that we grew up with, that stunts our internal growth. It's not
that we necessarily grew up with mean parents, but not all ways of
thinking are healthy for all people, even within the same family.

How many times have we made a gesture in fun only to find
out that it cut like a knife. Our thoughtless acts can hurt someone
we care for deeply. When this happens we are devastated. Sometimes it is such a blunder that we can never take it back. The words
we spoke in anger, our misconduct, or our actions can be a source
of permanent heartache.

For years my mother was a single parent raising four girls alone.
One evening, when I was around ten years old, my mother sat in
her favorite chair tired from a long day at work. She looked ex-

hausted and could hardly stay awake. I asked her "Mama, why do you work so hard?" She smiled at me and said, "So, you can live in a nice house, and have plenty of food to eat." Though I said nothing, her words really shook me. In my mind I interpreted her words to mean that her being tired was *my* fault. If I weren't around she wouldn't have to worry about the house and food; therefore she wouldn't have to work so hard. That's a lot of responsibility for a small child.

Our belief system is very similar. We tell ourselves things that aren't true; we buy into negative belief thinking. The problem is many times what we believe isn't the truth at all but our interpretation of the truth.

Believing in Myself

When we try to break old patterns, our whole being wants to reject it. As we go through our growing cycles in Feng Shui we will discover that our old thinking will try many times to block our way. We can break through these barriers, by being aware that they exist. The way we think about situations does in fact stifle our desire to manifest new things in our life.

The only thing that can keep you from your desire is your beliefs. If we don't accept the idea that we "deserve" our desire, then we will never even know it has happened even when it falls in our lap. What makes dreams come true? Believing that they will. This can be difficult when you have had the "nough" syndrome all your life. "Nough" syndrome: I'm not tall enough, pretty enough or smart enough.

Mighty Myra
Myra had won an election in a power position with the UAW. She is the first female to ever win this high a position in her region. This woman is a mother of six grown children. She loves casual clothes, bright colors and flowers, a far cry from the corporate image that this position demanded. When asked what she contributed to her success, the answer was simple

and to the point, "I made up my mind two years ago that I was going to have this position!" When I asked her if she ever had doubts, she said she did but when that "stinkin' thinkin" came to her she; dismissed it quickly.

To this gal negative thoughts were considered "stinkin' thinkin" and each time they entered her thoughts, she replaced them with how it would "feel" when she got her new position. This is one lesson in self belief we can all learn.

I believe in the me of myself.

The process is to discover your deepest desire and act upon it in a positive way. Your desires in life are crucial in your total comprehension of Feng Shui. Feng Shui is about all the parts that make up the whole. That whole is you.

Your life desires can be accomplished when we take the vital steps to reach them. Remember, the Universe wants to share its bounty and Spirit loves to give gifts. Believe in dreams and your right to own them. Your dreams are the truest gift of all—gifts of the heart.

Exercise:

Think for a moment about your dream. Then write a short story, one to one and half pages, as if you were writing about someone other then yourself. Tell why this person deserves this dream to come true.

Program students please complete the Knowing the Truth Work sheet Number 1101-5; Dreams and Desires Work sheet Number 1101-6 and 1101-7

Music to My Heart

Steps to Reaching your Truest Desire

Step One. Find it
Narrow your search using the nine life situations of Feng Shui; Work, Helping Friends and Travel, Children and Creativity, Relationships, Reputation, Riches, Family and Health, Knowledge and Self

Step Two. Consider it
Imagine all the aspect of your dream. Think about how it will look, feel and sound. Think about where you will be when it happens. How it will affect your life and the lives of those around you.

Step Three. Word it
Choose words that clearly describe your heart's desire. Focus on it and keep it always in front of you.

Step Four. Affirm it
Use your beautiful words to state out loud your dream in the positive. Turn statements into music that sings the songs of your dream and it birthing.

Step Five. Believe it
Believe that dreams come true because you deserve it. Relax in the certainty that Spirit always delivers an authentic heart's desire. Always be grateful and remember to say, "Thank you."

Wisdoms

The Car Room

Purpose:

The ideal situation is to drive into an oasis that you create for yourself out of the garage: an attractive place that leaves the chi energy strong and nurturing all day.

Suggestions:

Begin by renaming the garage the car room. Make it a real room by painting the walls, hanging art work and carpet or paint the floor.

Symbols:

Chaotic rooms symbolize life as out of control. Organization supports a well managed home. Well-lit car rooms draw chi through the garage door. Paint the outside of the door a color that blends with the house.

Color:

Green denotes energizing and blue supports serenity. Decorative shades of grays add effortless flow supporting a content family.

Understanding Our Reflection

The movie Alice and Wonderland was a childhood favorite of mine. I sat in awe as Alice stepped through the looking glass, going from adventure to adventure and meeting the most interesting people. The lessons were old ones that I had been taught before, but now they were reinforced by Alice and her pals. The Mad Hatter taught her to take time for herself, to indulge in life's simplest of pleasures, like that of taking tea. White Rabbit was obsessed with never being late and the Cheshire Cat always left behind the shadow of his smile, an idea more of us should do these days. Accepting who you are inside and allowing it to reflect on who you are on the outside was the underlying moral.

Reflecting Life's Aspirations

We seem to keep a lot of mirrors around our homes, though most would agree that looking in to them isn't the most popular of past times. It is amazing how in the first few moments after awakening we can appear so distorted. I personally don't make the transition between sleep and wakening very well at all! The way we see ourselves is usually much different then the person we see staring back at us from a mirror.

In Feng Shui we are taught that our lives are a mirror image of who we are. In another words, what we think about ourselves is reflected in the items we keep around us. It is important to live with things you love. Keeping things around you that translate in to glorious memories tell the chi that you love and care for yourself.

Now you are ready to look at how the spaces we choose to live in can reflect situations in your life.

I have seen many life situations mimicked in a home through damage, neglect, structural problems, leaks and wrong placement. These can cause devastating effects on people's lives — whether they are aware of it or not. It is very important that we pay close attention to those spaces that surround our lives.

Life inside the Qualities

There has always been a way to tell where in life you were at by a time line situation. For example, we say folks are in the prime of their life, under forty or in their twilight years, or over seventy. We can be hippies, yuppies or baby boomers. These "tags" tell us where in the life cycle we fit.

In Feng Shui there are life situations that are called qualities or treasures. These qualities are used to define what is happening to you in a present moment. We are in one of these qualities at every minute of every day. There are nine in all and they are: career, helpful people, children, relationships, fame, wealth, health, knowledge and the center.

Each "Quality of Life", as I like to call them, tells you what is occurring to you at any given time. You get up in the morning and go to work; you would be in the career quality. Going to the doctor, the health area ; or paying bills that day you would be in the wealth area. The key is to begin to recognize what "quality" you are in at that moment so that when things are not going your way you can check that the chi is not being blocked, thus correcting problems, even before they occur.

The qualities have many aspects to them and include things that we encounter on a daily basis.

By understanding the characteristics of each "quality" we begin to take back the control of our lives.

Career

Career, direction or journey is the part of our life that adds adventure. It is simply your job or the yearning for a new job. If your retired its the next step that life's journey has in store for you. It could be discovering your life's "work".

The direction of our life can take an entire lifetime to find, it can happen at any time or not at all. Sometimes discovering your life's work, or purpose, is like an deep secret that needs to be uncovered within the depth of us. It is looking into the true identity of who we want to be and discovering the steps to get there.

You are in the Career Quality or situation when:
At your current job or workplace
Looking for a new job
Volunteering or doing community work
Moving from one career to another
Giving up a career
Following your inner essence or passion

Helpful People

Helpful people also includes travel. This is because the real help in our lives takes place when their is action on our part. Movement denotes change and change is what helping is all about. Just rearranging a few things can give an new perspective on life in general. Helpful people are blessings when the world gets us down and there is no place to turn. Just like a kind face and a smile can lift up our spirits and guide us in a new direction.

You are in the Helpful People Quality
any time you help another

You are in the Helpful People and Travel Quality when:
Trying to refinance your house
Wanting to travel abroad
Driving anywhere
Looking for a good college
Wanting to move
Attracting more clients or customers

Children

Children and creativity are both included in this part of your life because in Feng Shui creativity comes from the courage of a child. Any artist will tell you that true originality comes from the little boy or girl who's imagination goes beyond conventional. The artistic person sometimes calls on the inner child to create beyond the realms of adulthood.

I know a wonderful artist named Emery Bear. He is well known for his paintings of angels, which he envisions with ease. It is with eyes of a child and the wonder of youth that he paints his life likes portraits of these celestial beings.

This "Quality of Life" supports all avenues of art including exercise, crafts, dance, martial arts, painting, drawing, sculpturing and sewing to name a few. Beside the creative side of us, it also includes all children and an environment geared at children, like toys stores. Your children, puppet theater, artwork depicting children and situations that concern actual children are also located in this sector.

You are in the Children and Creativity Quality when:
Trying to have children
Working on relating to your own children
Working with children in any capacity
Being creative or working on creative projects
Wanting to diminish creative blocks

Love

Love, marriage and intimacy are all avenues of life commonly called relationships. This includes any type of relationship from romantic love to coworker friendships. There are many different types of relationships. You have one type of relationship with your friends, another with the butcher. The way you feel about your community is different then you feel about your spouse. The love of self, enrichment and personal growth are also maintained in this area of your life.

You are in the Love and Relationship Quality when:
Trying to attract more love in you life of any kind
Looking for your soul mate
Developing a healthy relationship with your self
Improve existing relationships
Working on issues of the "heart"

Fame

Fame and reputation is how the world in general views you. It can include your position in the community, being honest in business, a great coach or simply the best third grade teacher in your elementary school. Whatever people think of you, or how you think of yourself, is in this quality. Matters of self-image, self-esteem and inner worth are all located here along with your reputation. Building an impeccable reputation gives us a good foot- hold in the community.

Where we live and work directly reflects back to us. This reflection should be supportive, honest and ready to help our neighbors. This secures base builds a sturdy future.

You are in the Fame and Reputation Quality when:
Striving for recognition at work
Looking for a promotion
Building a public image
To heighten your community reputation
In any volunteer position like coaching or instructing

Wealth

Wealth, riches, abundance and prosperity are phrases that are attached to this quality. The flow of money and the direction of personal finances are related here. Feng Shui is based on the belief that the best form of security is based on the principle of steady growth and accumulation. Therefore forms of prosperity are attracted to our lives when all things have equal importance.

Money matters to us not because it is so important, but that is isn't important enough. Most times we are much to eager to give away our hard-earned dollars. We think of it as a reward for a job well done. We work so hard for it, just to let it go for some frivolity that we didn't even want or need. Did you know that spending to much money is a form of self abuse? Working to spend is an out of control cycle that most folks would love to end. Slowly building wealth builds the momentum of riches through the gradual collecting of money.

I have a friend that told me once, "A lot of people have collections. Some collect stamps, others perhaps bells or dolls, but I collect money. It is one collection where you always know its true value".

All aspects of our lives that even hints at finances, money, riches, abundance and prosperity fits into this category.

You are in the Wealth and Abundance Quality when:
Wanting to produce more cash in your life
Raising funds for a charity or an event
Trying to generate cash for a specific need
Wanting to hold on to money longer
Paying bills
Going to the bank
Investments, savings, antiques, etc.
Collections
Buying an expensive gift
Items that were previously owned by affluent people

Health

Health and family make up the next life situation. Cultivating strong physical health and loving family ties is an interconnected foundation that keeps life at the highest quality. All health related topics are placed under this category, even something as simple as going to the health food store. Health work, healthy foods, exercise, medical conditions, and the prevention of them are all under this quality. Family plays a large role in this quality because in order to maintain extreme health our support system needs to be in tack. The healthier your family ties, the more balanced your overall wellness. Family, friends and pets are all connected to this area.

You are in the Family and Health Quality when:
Spending time with family or friends

At a party
You are at a doctor or dentist appointment
At the gym or competing in sports
Conducting any healthy activity
Spending time with your pet

Knowledge

Knowledge, spirituality, self-cultivation and enrichment are all part of this quality. In Feng Shui we are taught that true knowledge comes from a peaceful mind and a still heart. In order to grasp the art of deep learning a quietness must first be obtained in the mind.

There are many ways to achieve this quiet heart; meditation, chanting, singing, praying, gardening and walking are forms of self-cultivation. Our belief system plays an important role as to what we are the most comfortable with, but one thing is certain. We learn the best when there is less stress!

You are in the Knowledge and Spirituality Quality when:
Writing letters, taking notes or journaling
Counseling, conducting enrichment studies
Reading, studying or listening
Take classes of any type
Going to church or synagogue
Creating more connection with inner peace
Practicing any belief system

Center

The center, core, Tao, fortunate blessings, yin and yang are all names given to this situation in our life. The Tao of our life is where we find ourselves stabilized and centered. It is the part of us that connects everything else. This is where we go to be balanced and allow all the avenues of our life to be either connected or set aside. It is said to be the yin and the yang, the place of all, the Tao, the way.

This area nurtures the soul. It is you and it is me. What I mean by that is the center "Quality of Life" is the one factor that connects all the other areas. It is the heart, where the blood of chi energies pumps through to all the other aspects of the Universe. This is the universal foundation that lets us know that we are a part of a bigger picture and when we are in balance, all is right with our world.

You are in the Center Quality when:
You need to slow down the pace.
Going through a life crisis.
You have the desire for peace and serenity
At those times you want to focus on yourself
Trying to stabilize any of the other "qualities of life."
Enhancing and bringing together your work and home life.

Exercise:
Right now, while reading this book what Quality of Life are you in? What quality will you be in when: cooking a meal? Visiting a friend?

Program students please complete the Understanding Our Reflection Work sheet Number 1102

Wisdoms

Living Room

Purpose:

The "living" room is the room that supports the life of the family. The way the outside world views you is summed up on how this room looks to others.

Suggestions:

Warm, intimate groups of furnishings suggest heartfelt conversations. Be sure you add living items here to denote that life is worth living. Whenever possible try to see the door from all seating

Symbols:

Add art that depicts what you love to do. Use your room; don't just save it for company. Use plants in the room to represent living "chi". Place colored bulbs to lift the chi in dreary corners.

Color:

Keep large pieces of furniture neutral. Use small amounts of navy blue or black to add power. Add colorful artwork and accessories. Green denotes growth and blue serenity add a little of both to nurture the family.

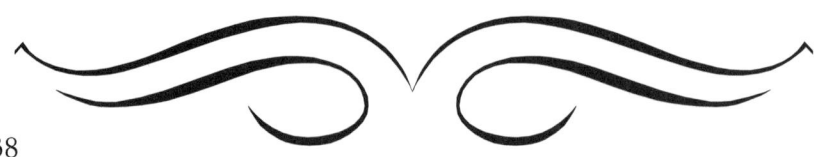

The Qualities
of Life

Through the study of Feng Shui, we can see the importance of how the qualities actually connect to your life. Daily activities put us in a quality even when we think we are doing nothing at all, we are. Let's say you jump in the car to drop off Aunt Sally's holiday package at the post office.

By following Feng Shui principles we are in helpful people and travel because we are driving *(travel)* to take a package to someone *(helpful people)* who insures to care for the bundle. The fact that it is going to *(family)* Aunt Sally it also includes health and family and depending on your intention could include relationships *(love)*.

The action we take while in certain situations affect their outcome. We can now begin to see how important it is to pay attention to those situations of life that we are in daily. The quality of our life actions is simply a process taking control of the outcome by being aware of the result.

This action does not have to be physical either. It can be a dream a desire or an intention.

An Example:
Mary Jane has been married for one year. Her husband works long hours and the evening meal has become their quiet time together. However, she would love to learn to cook more of varieties of foods to enhance this special time that they share.

Let's take a look at this situation. It isn't really action because Mary Jane has not taken any cooking classes yet, but she wants to. This is when the intent or desire is just as strong as the action. Mary Jane has been married one year. Her husband works long hours and the evening meal has become their quiet time together (love). However, she would love to learn to cook (knowledge) a variety of foods to enhance this special time that they share.

Recognizing situations

The above case is an example of where the intention is as strong as the action. Recognizing what situation, or part of our life, will be affected allows that area to be supported, or not supported, depending on the desire. Even if the action does not take place the situation or quality is still based on the individuals intention.

When you take the time to look any instance that happens in a day, and relate it one of the nine qualities, this recognition becomes power. It lets you become aware as to why certain things happen the way they do. Sometimes a routine task can go haywire making no sense to you. Seeing where in the "qualities of life" these situations fall gives you the tools to make the necessary adjustments before a problem exists.

Learning to take a situation that is needed, and breaking it down into the pertinent "quality" is a usable tool. Adding other qualities that support each other will further support the intention giving it more dimension. The deeper the layers, the more complete the results.

The qualities characteristics

Once we learn to recognize which quality we are in during a given situation the next step is to know all the aspect of that quality or treasure. Each "Quality of Life " or "Life Treasures", as they are sometimes called, has associations attached to it that symbolically represent the life situation. By comprehending these associations we are better equipped to know where they fit in our life. When a life situation happens we are able to take the circumstances and apply them to the proper quality.

Each of the nine qualities has characteristics that make them unique to themselves. Just like we have features that set us apart, so do life situations. Many things happen to us in any given day, sometimes it's easy to tell what quality is involved. Other times the answer isn't as clear.

When we learn the attributes we can better reason where situations fit into Feng Shui. If we were to describe a situation we are able to tell what quality is present without actually seeing it. For example, if I were to describe a man I saw as a *gentleman, wearing a long black robe with a white color and crucifix around his neck*. You would correctly reason him as some type of clergy. Then upon reviewing the "Qualities of Life" you would categorizes him as belonging to the knowledge and spirituality quality.

Quality associations

The "Qualities of Life" have descriptions that identify them as well. Since qualities themselves are not tangible, we add physical descriptions to them through the use of symbolism. By using both the symbol and the characteristic, we now create sensible qualities that we can actually see.

The quality of career is considered a journey, the next step in our life work, one that flows. It is related to the curvy, flow of a river full of excitement and surprises. The adjectives curvy, flow and the representation of water are all attributes of the quality of life we call career and direction.

Words and descriptions are powerful symbols of the actual life situation or quality. By adding them to the attribute, personal symbols enrich the quality even more. When you combine a personal symbol to any quality, you are enhancing the effectiveness of the chi being drawn to that situation. A personal symbol adds your personal chi to a situation, thus adding strength in clarifying the end result. As we talked about discovering your wants and desires take some thought. Once your are focused on the desire and the reason you want it, personal symbols then link the enormous power of the universe to your desire, allowing them to materialize in your life.

Marvelous Melissa

Melissa was told that the company she was working for was down sizing and her position would be phased out. She turned to Feng Shui so that as she sent out her resume' the chi would support her in finding a new job. Melissa wasn't exactly sure what she wanted to do, but she knew she wanted to work in an office, and needed to find it before the other job ended.

We ascertained that the qualities to work on were career and helpful people. Career was for the actual job and helpful people to help her find the position quickly. We began discussing ways to draw the chi to the quality that would give the clear message of what she wanted. I suggested that she use the color black, because this was one of colors associated to career, and add a personal symbol to strengthen her needs. Melissa had a photo of herself wearing a business suit that she placed in a contemporary black frame. Next to it she had a little clock with a black face. The clock was ideal because it would keep the chi moving steadily. Within thirty days Melissa had five interviews and got that great new job. Today she enjoys her position as office manager and owes it all to her "good" Feng Shui.

Each characteristic is important in itself and has as much influence as any of the others. Though the one used the most often is color, all the attributes should be considered when using them to balance or as an adjustment in a space. There are times when an item is needed and color can't be considered, either through personal taste or decor.

Each aspect of a quality supports a situation in our life, whether tangible or intangible. Just like no single part of an attribute that describes us is more important than another. Neither are the attributes of the "Qualities of Life". Some characteristics will mean more to different people. That is because certain aspect of personality we are naturally drawn to. For example some people are drawn to a beautiful smile, while others love the twinkle in mischievous eyes. A "Quality of Life" and its attributes are divided into in parts. These parts are; title, number, natural phenomena, season, animal, color, gem, and fabric and personal symbols.

Quality Title

The title of a quality is the name given it through the philosophy of Feng Shui. As we talked about in the first part of this book it is important that our intention is clear. Each quality is given a name but it also has other associations related to it. These are based on Western language and philosophy. For example: career can mean the job you are working at now, a job you'd like to have, or no job at all. It can also mean a new direction in life, and adventure or a journey. All the qualities have a mirrored of association to them.

The Number

There is an entire science behind the numbers associated to the each quality in Feng Shui. Knowing the number associated to the qualities of life will increase your accuracy when activating a particular sector.

Many of the numbers in Feng Shui make sense to our Western thinking but some do not. The number two is related to love, this we understand because we relate the number two as being a pair or a couple. Health and family use the number three which can relate to a family; father, mother and child. Helpful people associate the number six to it which is not relevant in our Western language. Since this is traditional Feng Shui it isn't as easy for us to understand. However, the number is just as powerful whether we fully undersigned the process or not.

Natural Phenomena

Many of the qualities have a natural counter part. In the career quality the natural symbol is the sea, which is significant because it represents water. Water represents the flow of life. Since our journey in life is the way we want our life to go it also symbolizes the natural acts that can occur. Each Natural phenomenon is individual in itself. The sea doesn't act like the sun and the sun doesn't act like a tree and so on. This association tells us how the quality should proceed.

Season

Four of the qualities have a season directly related to them the others are combinations of the seasons. Our life goes through cycles very similar to the season's cycles. Career is related to our direction so it becomes important that we hibernate drawing our chi to us while we are contemplating our journey. This associates to winter.

Autumn is a time for the anticipation of things to come it relates to children. Summer is full of movement and action. It radiates with fun and aliveness its association is summer. Health and family with all its new growth and birthing represent the freshness in our life. This wholesome newness is related to spring.

Animal, Color, Gems Fabric

Each quality is associated to an animal, its own color, a stone, a fabric and other items. This association is based on the seasons and the natural phenomena. They are based on the elements of the earth and can entail many similar items. When used in combination these can magnify an intention drawing even healthier chi. For example, associated to Children and Creativity are: The number: seven, Animal: Tiger Color: white & pastels Stones: Mother of Pearl. So, a perfect gift for a creative loved one would be a bracelet with seven tigers, carved out of mother of pearl.

Personal Symbols

When you use personal symbols the item then represent a quality within you. Symbols are a kind-of logo, telling the Universe what you are all about. Some symbols are obvious, a building in a city might represent a new job, or a sunset might mean reflection on your path in life. Others are very personal an may take on the meaning of a family heritage, or other process that has deep significance to you.

My friend Cheryl bought some men's shaving cream, a toothbrush and a razor and put them in the relationship area of her bathroom. This was her way of telling the Universe what she wanted and reinforcing it with a symbol in the appropriate section of her home. Must of worked, she was married eighteen months later.

The qualities and their descriptions

Each quality has a list of characteristics and descriptions that help us determine how to use them in our life. Some of these descriptions we can reason out others we must learn because they carry a much deeper meaning. Let's review the attributes of each quality and what they convey to the Universe about your intention.

Career

Life Direction, Adventure, Enterprise
Animal — Tortoise
Color — Black/Navy Blue
Number — #1
Element — Water
Season — Winter
Body Area — Ears
Shapes — Free forms, asymmetrical

Personal Symbols
- Water features such as fountains, waterfalls and aquariums.
- Pictures of streams, oceans, lakes, waterfalls, ponds, etc.
- Images that represent your career and direction goals.
- Items in black; and dark tones such as eggplant and navy.
- Mirrors, glass, foil, Mylar, and crystal.
- Items from companies where you'd like to work.

Helpful People and Travel

Circulate, Service, Benefactors
Color — Gray
Number — #6

Element — Water and Metal
Season — Late Autumn
Body Area — Head
Shapes — Circle, oval, arch, asymmetrical, free flowing, winding

Personal symbols

- Pictures taken while traveling, or artwork of places you want to travel.
- Art depicting means of travel: boats, cars, planes, carriages, and trains.
- Items in the colors of white, gray and black.
- Photos of teachers, mentors, benefactors, clients, customers, and employees.
- Places that are special to you in the world.

Children and Creativity

Inner Child, Genius, Originality, Novelty
Animal — Tiger
Color — White/Pastels
Number — #7
Element — Metal
Season — Autumn
Body Area — Mouth
Shape — Circle, oval and arch

Personal symbols

- Pictures of children, artwork created by children, handmade items and crafts.
- Whimsical items, dolls and stuffed toys.
- The colors of white, off white, and pastels.
- Things made from metals such as gold, silver, brass, wrought iron, etc.
- Stones such as quartz, marble, granite, and malachite.

Love and Marriage

Partnership, Marriage, Relationships
Color — Pink, Yellow (pastels)
Number — #2
Element — Fire and Metal
Special Symbol — Motherhood
Body Area — Organs
Shapes— Triangles, pyramids, cones, circles, ovals.

Personal symbols
- Pictures of your partner or your desired partner.
- Items in pairs, such as lovers, doves, dolphins, hearts, flowers and lace.
- Artwork of famous lovers: Venus, Aphrodite, Don Juan, Cupid, etc.
- Items in the colors of red, pink and white.
- Romantic mementos, gifts given to you by a lover, wine bucket, silky fabrics, etc.

Fame and Reputation

Recognition, Notoriety, Status, Honor
Animal — Bird, Phoenix
Color — Red
Number — #9
Element — Fire
Season — Summer
Body Area — Eyes
Shapes — Triangles, pyramids or cones

Personal Symbols
- Diplomas, awards, prizes, and acknowledgments.
- Things made from animals, such as leather, feathers, wool and bone.

- Pictures of pets, animals, people, celebrities, mentors.
- Items in the red color spectrum.
- Artwork with the sun, fireplaces or sunshine.
- Triangular, conical, and pyramid shaped items
- Sunlight, candles, electrical lights, oil lamps, etc.

Wealth and Abundance

Prosperity, Resources, Advantage, Comfort
Color — Purple
Number — #4
Body Area — Hip/Bones
Element — Fire and Wood
Shapes — Triangle, cone, pole, columnar and stripes

Personal symbols

- Crystal, valuable accessories, collections, antiques, art, sculpture, coins.
- Rich fabrics such as velvet, lamé, silk, moiré, and damask
- Pictures that depict expensive items such as homes, cars, boats and jewelry.
- Items in the colors of purple, violet or lavender, green, blue and red.
- Colors that sound rich like ruby red, emerald green, silver, gold and platinum.
- Water features, such as fountains and waterfalls, symbolizing the abundant flow of money and prosperity.
- Actual money, stocks, bonds, mutual funds, insurance paperwork, etc

Health and Family

Friends, Exercise, Ancestry, Origin, Birth
Animal — Dragon
Color — Green & Blue
Number — #3
Element — Wood
Season — Spring
Body Area — Feet
Shapes — Columnar, poles and stripes

Personal symbols

◆ Art of sport figures, family, pets, friends, gardens and landscapes.
◆ Items in the colors of blue and green.
◆ Things made of wood, including furniture and decorations.
◆ Healthy plants and flowers (real, silk or images of these).
◆ Mementos, awards, heirlooms, bowls of fruit, items from family members.

Knowledge and Spirituality

Education, Wisdom, Counseling, Mentor
Color — Turquoise and Teal
Number — #8
Body Area — Hands
Shapes — Free forms, asymmetrical, winding, columnar, poles and stripes

Personal symbols

◆ Study materials, books, tapes, and papers.
◆ Pictures of serene places, mountains and quiet places.

- Figures of teachers, spiritual deities, guides, gods, goddesses, saints, and angels.
- Things in the colors of teal, turquoise, black, blue, and green.
- Items used for self-enrichment: journals, diaries, etc.

Yin/Yang, Core

Center, Hub, Root, Soul, Essence, Whole, Fortunate Blessings.
Yin/Yang — Connects all eight sections
Color — Yellow or Earth Tones
Number — #5
Body Part — Back, Spinal Column

Personal symbols

- Art depicting the world, stars and the celestial heavens.
- Pictures of land, soil, dirt, deserts, the beach, etc.
- Heavy or dense objects, items made of concrete, clay, sand, resins, etc.
- Things in the colors of yellow, brown, and earth-tones.
- Symbols representing solidity or stability in your life.

As you explore the "Qualities of Life" and their attributes, you begin to see the endless possibilities through their own descriptions and the use of personal symbols. Personal symbols, or mementos are tangible affirmations that are not only visual, but have immense emotion attached to them. They are private mantras that hold special meaning; ones that leave you with feelings of great joy. This great joy gives the Universal energies a clear picture of what is needed in your life situation.

Exercise:
In the below life situation choose the best; Quality Of Life, attribute and personal symbol. Situation: Needing extra money for college.

Program students please complete the Qualities of Life Work sheet Number 1103

Tip

Fix any flooring that is loose or defective. The path in which we walk carries with it our dreams.

Wisdoms

Dining Rooms

Purpose:

The sacred ritual of partaking meals in many cultures translates "I love you" into, "I will cook for you." Reclaim this space to enhance both food for body and food for thought.

Suggestions:

To announce dinnertime create a ceremony like setting the table. Choose draperies that close to avoid distractions. Create atmosphere with music and lighting.

Symbols:

Solid linens help minds to stay on the conversation. Keep center-pieces short to be able to see over them easily. Avoid clock or guest may feel they have to eat and run. Botanicals, lankscapes and pottery are the best artwork for this area.

Color:

Bright colors such as yellow and orange add a festive style. Pinks and rose promote quiet conversation. Blue will soothe frazzled nerves. Nuetrals work best for business dinners.

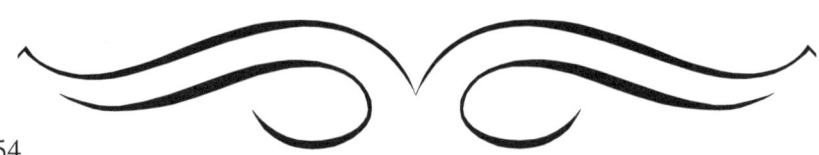

Our
Bodies

One of the underlying factors in Feng Shui is how these quali ties relate to us personally. This is not limited to just emo-tionally, but it also affects us physically. The relationship between our mind, body, and spirit is interconnected. When one area is unbalanced, it throws the whole system out of harmony.

When a life situation happens to us, many times it will manifest itself in the form of pain or tenderness in our body. This manifes-tation can happen even when the situation you are currently in is good. Have you ever been so excited about a wonderful upcoming event that you ended up with a headache or stomach pain? Most of us have. That is because the chi energy associated to that par-ticular life situation very personally affects us deeply!

As you work through life situations, and strengthen them sym-bolically in your home, don't forget to do a personal check on your body. Balanced harmony can only be complete when we are at our optimum, recognizing what to look at on the outside will help take care of the inner Feng Shui.

Here are a few ways the body can reflect the chi energy around us:

If you cry a lot, have sinus problems, kidney infections, urinary, bladder or any type of reproduction problems ask yourself: "Do I like my job? Is there another direction I should be taking? Is life an adventure to me?"

If your feet ache, have bunions, corns, warts, or other forms of foot disorders, ask yourself: "How well do I get along with my family? How is my overall health? Do I take good care of myself?"

If you bite your finger nails, have pain in finger joints, calluses on the palms of your hands or any disorder with your fingers, hands, or wrist, ask yourself: "What do I think about myself? How do others look at me?"

If you have pain in your elbows or shoulders, difficulty with dislocated shoulders, bruising to the collar bone, or inflammation in the shoulder blades, ask yourself: "Do I have a good support system? Am I willing to reach out for help when I need it?"

If you have reoccurring chest pains, high blood pressure, pounding or ringing in your ears, or any type of pulmonary disorder, ask yourself: "Do I have a good relationship with my significant other? Do I love and accept myself completely?"

If you have frequent flues, colds, congestion, pleurisy, or other breathing disorders, back pain or other back problems, ask yourself: "Am I as creative as I want to be? Is my inner child going unnoticed? Do I have difficulty accepting that I am a parent?"

If you have acid reflux, heartburn, sour stomach, distorted taste buds or high acid in the body, ask yourself: "How are my finances? How do I really feel towards money? Do I get great opportunities coming my way?"

If you suffer from ulcers, acid stomach, poor digestion, frequent headaches, inconsistent elimination, or lower back pain, ask yourself: "Do I worry a lot? How well do I finish tasks? Am I good at resolving conflicts?"

If you get leg cramps, muscle spasms, suffer from depression or feeling "low", ask yourself: "Am I flexible, can I see both sides? Am I tense or relaxed?"

Each quality or life situation has a reference point in our body. These can work together for a strong wellness program, or against each other causing conflict. At times you can alert yourself to a potential problem in your life by simply paying attention to how your body reacts in a certain situation.

Body Part	*Quality Of Life*
Kidneys:	Career, Direction and Journey
Feet:	Family, Health, and Growth
Hands:	Fame, Reputation, and Values
Arms:	Helpful People, and Travel
Heart:	Love, and Relationships
Lungs:	Children, Creativity, Inner Child
Stomach:	Support, Stability, Foundation
Small Intestine:	Wealth, Finances, and Fortune
Ankles and Calves:	Knowledge and Spirituality

The Qualities of Life and the Body

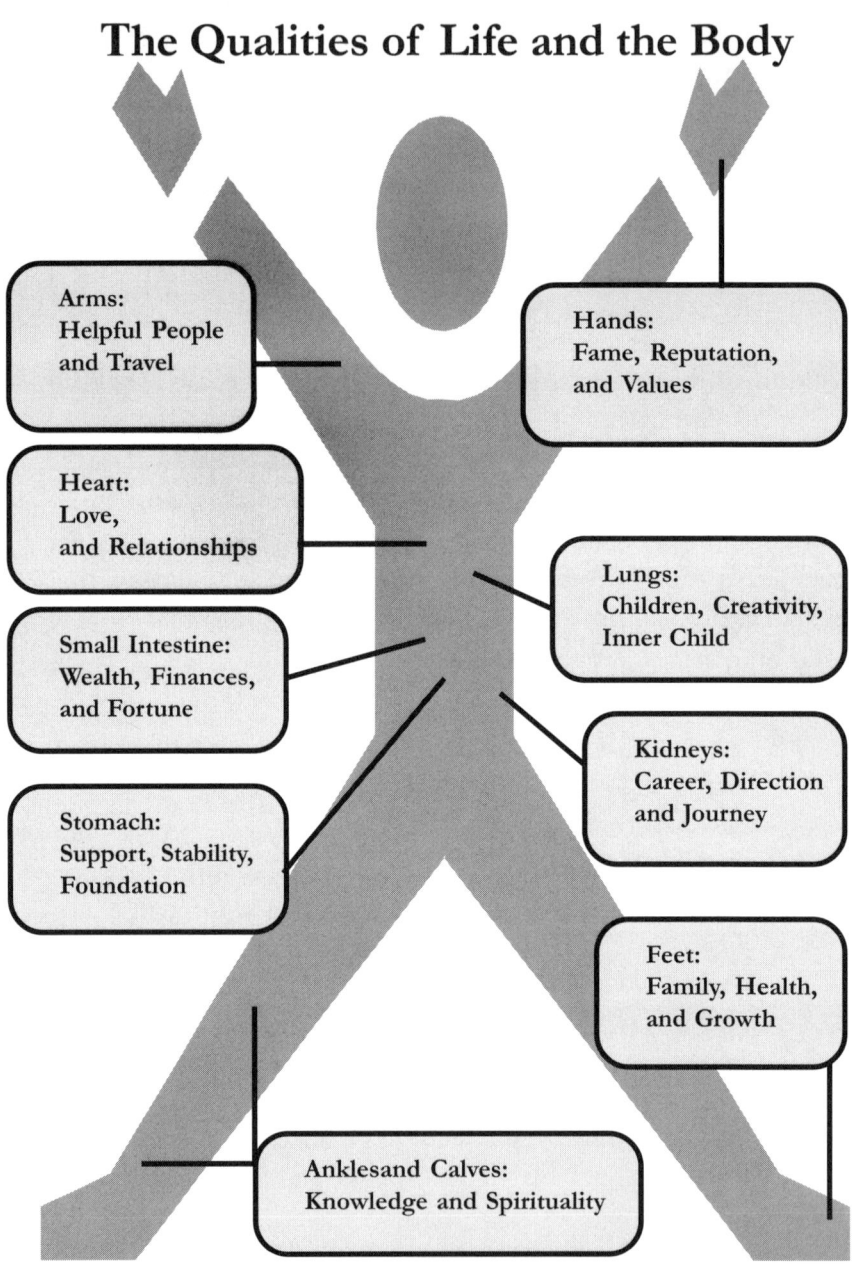

Arms:
Helpful People
and Travel

Hands:
Fame, Reputation,
and Values

Heart:
Love,
and Relationships

Lungs:
Children, Creativity,
Inner Child

Small Intestine:
Wealth, Finances,
and Fortune

Kidneys:
Career, Direction
and Journey

Stomach:
Support, Stability,
Foundation

Feet:
Family, Health,
and Growth

Anklesand Calves:
Knowledge and Spirituality

Chi affects everything around us. Sometimes we get so caught up in adjusting our home we forget that the reason for doing Feng Shui in the first place is to improve our lives. Your life is improved when you allow your personal chi to resonate. When this happens, the natural chi works in harmony, drawing to it all that is perfection.

Tip

When trying to loose weight avoid entering the home through the kitchen.

Section II

Wisdoms

Master Bedroom

Purpose:

The bedroom is the most personal room in the house. It is our ultimate inner sanctum; where we go to rejuvenate. Naturally you want the room to reflect your true spirit.

Suggestions:

Remove all clutter. Use natural items as much as possible. The bed should be firmly against the wall. Keep accessories at a minimum. Hang landscapes that make you feel cozy.

Symbols:

Add art that depicts love of self and love of another. Use items in pairs to denote a couple or three to represent family. Be careful not to fill the bed with toys, and pillows.

Color:

Use colors such as peach, gold, warm blues and greens. To draw romance use red in small amounts. Purple adds mystery. Pinks supports intimacy and youth.

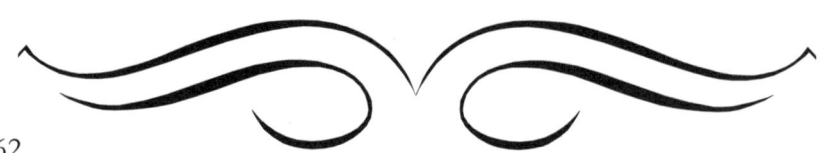

Chapter 5

Reflecting Earth

There is something about the solitude of being alone in the woods. When life gets me down, I love to walk and think in a woodland area near my home. This sanctuary for deer, fox, raccoons, rabbits, and a number of birds, chipmunks and squirrels is the place I find the peace to calm my thoughts. The early morning reminds me - I need this deep connection to nature. The indentation of the grass where a deer has spent the night and the newly dug holes made by the moles tell me that this place is alive with earth energy. Not only am I able to balance myself, but I'm increasing my personal chi. Of all the things I do to center myself, this is my most favorite.

Natural energies are present everywhere: in the woods, on the beach, in the mountains, and even in our own backyards. Honoring their existence adds dimension to the energy that is present there.

**As living beings, we find it necessary to
replenish our life with other living things.**

Some of us find this contentment in nature itself; others are able to symbolically nurture ourselves with flower arrangements, paintings, and pets. Either way, we are a world that keeps its roots deeply seeded in the earth.

We are children of the Earth. Our sheer existence depends on this planet and what she provides. Our shelters are constructed with a combination of wood, earth and metal. Our food is vegetation that grows in her soil; animals eat the vegetation to provide food and clothing. Water gives us life and power. The list is endless of how the Earth provides for our physical existence. The Earth energies also provide us with a powerful chi, that when mixed with man's chi, complete the law of universal energies.

I love the interaction between the earth energies, heaven and our own chi. They are so subdued, and so quiet, that many times we fail to notice the enormous power they hold. When we use the tools that the Universe provides, we are actually walking in the energies themselves. This has a dynamic effect on you. Working with Earth energies through Feng Shui can single-handedly change your life forever.

Our interaction with nature

Different features of the Earth emit a different type of chi from them. The ingredients of the feature itself cause variations in the chi. These can be felt depending on where you are. There is the sense of renewal in the woods, the sizzle and excitement of the beach, serenity near the water, contemplation in the mountains, and a feeling of wholeness when we are alone in nature.

The early Chinese knew the importance of the Earth for survival and revered the land for providing their livelihood. The origins of Feng Shui are based firmly in the Earth energies, and originate out of survival and spiritual rite. Through this pragmatic approach, demographic features were used to represent the chi energies attached to them. The tree represented the nurturing soul; the sun depicts illumination; and mountains feel the full force of heaven; the sea-life's effortless course; and soil the force of Mother Earth.

These five features: tree, sun, mountains, sea, and soil represent nature and should be used, when possible, in their natural state.

Feng Shui is rooted in the harmony that is found in nature. We need a balance of all five elements in order to keep our chi energies at their highest. How can we do this? It would be impossible, or at least impractical, to have a mountain in the middle of our living room. So, we symbolically add these features to our spaces by incorporating building blocks called the elements.

There are five elements that correspond to their natural counterparts. These five elements are: wood, fire, metal, water, and earth; and have a wide range of characteristics associated to them. These five fantastic ingredients can be used for anything from stabilizing a space to selecting the right carpet color.

It's Elemental, My Dear

We are beginning to embark on my passion — the elements. I truly believe that one of the reasons my clients have effective consultations is because they have learned the art of balancing the elements. By using these wondrous tools you will begin to know where to tap into, when you want to heighten a space. Each of the five elements has a full range of associations, including color, shapes, and accessories that form the vocabulary for observing and governing them.

The Elements:

Wood
Fire
Metal
Water
Earth

The elements, Mother Nature's symbolic graces

The most efficient way to learn the "dance" of the elements is to practice using them in your home and every other chance you can. Through this continued practice, you will become proficient in the use of these fantastic gems. Each element has several attributes associated to it. There is the actual element itself, the natural counterpart, items made from the element, and things that symbolically represent the element.

Attributes of the Elements

Wood: Trees
- Items: trees, flowers and plants (real, dried, or silk)
- Colors: green and blue
- Shapes: columnar shapes, stripes (either horizontal or vertical)
- Decorative Features: Wooden furniture, decks, siding, beams, pedestals, banisters, and accessories made of wood. Linen, cotton, and other plant-based textiles. Paintings or pictures of woods, woodlands, trees, or art depicting any of the above.

Fire: The Sun
- Items: fireplaces, electrical lights, candles and stoves
- Colors: all shades of red and orange
- Shapes: triangles, pyramids, cones and diamonds

- Decorative Features: People, pets and animals. Items made from animals, bone, leather, wool, and silk. Pictures of the sun, or art depicting any of the above.

Metal: Mountains
- Items: all metals; silver, gold, bronze, etc.
- Colors: white and pastels
- Shapes: round, half rounds, swags, curves, circles
- Decorative Features: Ores such as marble, granite, and natural crystals. Photos of mountains, or art depicting any of the above.

Water: The Sea
- Items: ponds, river streams, lakes, oceans
- Color: black or navy
- Shapes: asymmetrical, winding and snakelike
- Decorative Features: Birdbaths, fountains, aquariums, cut glass, mirrors, chandeliers. Bowls of water, reflective surfaces, Mylar or moiré fabrics. Water scenes, or art depicting any of the above.

Earth: Soil
- Items: land, dirt, sand, etc.; objects made of the earth
- Colors: earth tones: brown, orange or yellow
- Shapes: rectangular or squares
- Decorative Features: Terra cotta, clay, ceramic, glass, earthenware, concrete, plaster, and things made from the Earth. Photos of the sky, global art, deserts, sandy beaches, and art that depicts any of the above.

Working with the Elements

As you begin to recognize the elements as accessories in your home, you will find that most homes are either missing or weakly portraying at least one element. The goal is to show all elements present in every room. Knowing how much of an element should be present in an area can be a challenge. It isn't necessary to have equal amounts of them, only that they are all present.

Rule #1: When elementally balancing a large area, begin by adding several small symbols: adding more later according to personal taste.

When an element needs balancing, begin by adding small quantities of the missing element. It is easier to bring in several small items rather than one large item. Each time you add an item in that element see how the room feels. Since one factor of yin and yang is based on personal taste, the amount of a particular element will also be personal.

Seattle Sue

Susan wanted to redesign the master bedroom in her new home. After following all the other Feng Shui principles, balancing the elements was next on her list. She removed the mirror from her room to keep the chi more restful. Since personal taste would not permit a fountain in the room, Susan had a dilemma. What other ways could she put back the water element in the room? Wood candle holders were replaced with cut glass ones. A picture frame and a potpourri bowl were crystal. A black throw pillow was added to an armchair. The finishing touch was a beautiful snow globe on the night table.

When using the elements, the factors to remember are; they all must be present and that they support the intentions of the individuals that live in the home. As you balance the elements in your home, you will see the results. Not only do rooms look great, they feel wonderful! Rooms that are elementally balanced take on a look of splendor and peace. Regardless of how large the room or how much money was spent on items, elementally balanced rooms transform the ordinary to extraordinary.

Rule #2: How much money you spend on decorating has nothing to do with how well a space can be elementally balanced. Begin using those items you truly love.

To balance a space begin by using things that you already own. Look at the items you have and decide how you really feel about the item. The goal is to be aware of the history, or the association of an item. Be certain that you love the object and that it supports what you want to accomplish in your life and in your family. Every object has at least one element associated to it most have more then one element. For example a round ceramic bowl of flowers has three elements attached to it. The shape of the bowl round represents metal, the ceramic symbolizes earth and the flowers contribute to the wood element.

When a room is elementally balanced, it resonates with vibrant chi and keeps all the energies in the house at the highest possible level. Working within a room is sometimes all you need to balance an entire space. When a space is out of balance, the occupants have trouble feeling grounded and may get easily confused.

Rule #3: <u>NEVER</u> wait to balance a space until you find the right decorative touch. Use another item that you love temporarily until you find that "special" item. The key is to <u>begin now</u>.

Though it is important to surround yourself with things you love, balancing your space is equally crucial. Many times we choose to wait to deal with our homes until we find just the right couch, area rug, or even the right house. Being dissatisfied with your surroundings is an indication of a deeper unhappiness.

Immovable Irene

Irene wanted to practice Feng Shui but wasn't sure where to begin. She read several books and even had a Feng Shui Home evaluation. Though many suggestions were made, she never made a single change. Her reasoning was that she didn't have the money or the time to make the changes. After investigating the problem a little further, Irene's original reason for wanting a consultation was because she felt stuck in life, unable to move ahead. Since our homes are a mirror image of what is happening inside us, hesitation and indecision may lead to uncertainty in corresponding life situations.

In the above case with Irene, we see a parallel between the lack of motivation using Feng Shui suggestions and her inability to move ahead in life. Feeling unable to move ahead, or in a rut, can cause the wheels of our intention to quit turning freely. In other words, our intention should never be stifled by inaction on our part.

No matter the reason, for whatever you want to accomplish in your life, begin today by balancing your space with the elements. Don't wait another day. Start to take charge of your life - now. Hold on to all that is precious, and reflect it back to the world through the loving affirmations called the elements.

Balancing the Elements

Balancing the elements is easy on a small scale by adding or subtracting accessories. However, at times certain elements can dominate a home — especially when used as an architectural feature. Some homes can have a strong wood element, such as wood floors, wood doors and trim, beams in the ceiling, wood cabinets, and furnishings. These can be difficult and expensive to change all at once.

When dealing with architectural features balance these situations by being aware of how the elements relate to each other. The elements interact with each other in primarily in two ways:

1. Nourishing and **2. Controlling.**

Nourishing

Nourishing cycles feed and sustain the elements in harmony. When trying to accomplish a situation in your life use the nourishing element will support that need. It doubles the effectiveness of an element you are working with by using the nourishing element to support it.

Nourishing cycle:

Water sustains Wood
Wood fuels Fire
Fire creates Earth
Earth produces Metal
Metal holds Water

Use the nourishing cycles when trying to produce more of a particular type of chi around you.

For example: *You'd like life to be more stable.*

How to use it: *Add earthenware pottery in your home in terra cotta or red. Pottery symbolizes earth; terra cotta color symbolizes fire. Thus, Fire creates Earth.*

Controlling

Using one element to control another element quiets or calms an area. Rooms that are heavy, or have too much of one element, loose their balance and cause the chi to stop moving in its natural pattern. To subdue a dominant element, use the controlling cycle.

Controlling cycle:

Wood consumes Earth
Earth dams Water
Water extinguishes Fire
Fire melts Metal
Metal cuts Wood

Use controlling elements when one element dominates a space, or to slow down the pace of the energies, especially when the feature cannot be removed.

For example: *Your home is made of stucco, you have ceramic tile and love earthenware. Lately you feel that life is at a standstill.*

How to Use: *To control the earth element, you add a wood mantel, large lush plants and several floral arrangements. Thus, Wood consumes Earth.*

Elemental Chi

In addition to the nourishing and controlling cycles, each element also carries with it a specific type of chi. Since certain elements stimulate certain types of chi, increasing the amount of a corresponding element will add support at those times when a particular need arises. This can be done after the space is balanced to lift the chi and point it towards a specific direction.

Wood symbolizes growth and new beginnings.
Fire stimulates action and motivation.
Earth balances and stabilizes the chi around us.
Metal is on the cutting edge; sharp and detailed.
Water represents effortless flow, a calm and sensitive path.

When we are able to attach not only a tangible item, something we can see, with a style of chi energy, how the space makes us feel, we can better utilize all aspects of the elements. Feng Shui teaches us that our glorious spaces should not just look great but touch us is a very peaceful manner.

Exercise:
Look around the room that you are currently in. Write down the first five things you see. Now assign an element to them.

Program students please complete the Reflecting Earth Worksheet Number 1205

Wisdoms

Family Room

Purpose:

The family room represents the bonding of people as one unit. It reflects nurturing, rebirth and health. It is where we go to relax, and spend quality time with our family.

Suggestions:

Comfortable, overstuffed furniture with lots of pillows and warm throws are the focus here. A good reading light and books within arms reach are a must.

Symbols:

Use pictures of loved ones, mementos and heirlooms. Avoid furniture that is cold to the touch; keep the room warm and comfy. Nature scenes or landscapes work best in this room.

Color:

Earth tones add a sense of stability and security.
Gold symbolizes wisdom and unity. Dark Green denotes devotion and unity

Designing Elements

The elements are useful in helping with decisions concerning decor. When you run into a snag during a decorating project, stop and do an element count. If you need new carpet, make a list of what elements are present and which ones the room needs. Perhaps the room is missing earth. The color choices you would then consider for carpet would be: brown, taupe, coffee, cocoa, yellow, cream with a yellow cast, orange, peach, or gold tones.

Need a new sofa? Let's pretend that the weakest element in the room is metal. Choose an off white couch with rounded arms and pillows. Want to hang the family pictures? Place them anywhere you need a little fire. It isn't necessary to implement decorative objects when using the elements, but what a great combination - influence and beauty!

Color

Using color as a chi magnet in a space will support the balance of the chi when following a developing sequence. Based on the cycle of nourishment and using the elements, color can be used as a foundation for your life through the reflection of your home.

**Use the colors associated with the elements
as a guideline when decorating.**

Begin with the floor as the foundation. Then choose the color for the walls, large pieces of furniture, window coverings, and finally, accents.

For example: In the dining room if you have white carpet, choose a cherry dining table, gray walls, tan draperies and blue white (ceiling white) paint for the ceiling.

White Carpet: metal
Cherry dining table: fire (cherry color)
Gray Walls: water
Tan draperies: earth
Blue white ceiling paint: wood

Room for Color

Color is not just supported by the direction of the cycle but also by adding it to the proper room. The chi in a room can be further enhanced when used in conjunction to the activities that go on in that room. The names we attach to rooms identify their purpose. The room in our home where we prepare food is commonly called the kitchen the room where e rest is the bedroom, and so on. The functions that take place in the individual rooms of our home produce their own chi and is strengthened by the color we use in them.

To use the element as color in a particular room first decide the purpose of the room. Is this where the family plays or studies? Second what type of foundation do you want to set -- stable, flowing or growing? Add the color that represents the type of foundation to the floor. Third surround the family by the element that supports the needs of the family by using these colors on the walls. Fourth use the colors of the other elements in the room to balance the chi throughout the house. Let's examine how this works.

Family Room

The purpose of the family room is to bring the family together. For family stability add earth to the floor. This is accomplished with flooring in the tones of tan, brown or gold. The element directly associated to family is wood, symbolizing nurturing and togetherness. This is added to the walls by shades of blue and green; the family will then be surrounded by the chi of growth and new beginnings. Metal, fire, and water are added in the way of furnishings and accessories to further balance the room. Since the element of wood is already present, because of the nature of the family room and the color of the walls, avoid adding more wood to this space in the way of patterns such as flowers, stripes, linen, and cotton.

The Room for Color Chart

There are numerous ways to set up your room elementally, and using color will dynamically enhance a room. The Room for Color chart on the next page is an easy guide for choosing the most effective color scheme and it will make selections easier. If your room is already set up try adding the associated colors through accessories and artwork.

Color activates the chi allowing it to move in an upward swing.

Room for Color Chart

	Floor	Walls and Trim	Furniture	Window Coverings	Accents	Avoid
Family Room	Tan, Brown, Gold	Blue, Green, Aqua, Teal	Off White, White, Beige	Rose, Red, Pink, Peach, Blush	Gray, Black, Navy, Eggplant	Florals, Stripes, Linen, Cotton
Living Room	Gray, Black, Navy, Eggplant	Tan, Brown, Gold	Blue, Green, Aqua, Teal	Off White, White, Beige	Rose, Red, Pink, Peach, Blush	Ceramic, Brick, Desert Art, Squares
Dinning Room	Blue, Green, Aqua, Teal	Off White, White, Beige	Rose, Red, Pink, Peach, Blush	Gray, Black, Navy, Eggplant	Tan, Brown, Gold	Marble, Granite, Bronze
Kitchen	Off White, White, Beige	Rose, Red, Pink, Peach, Blush	Gray, Black, Navy, Eggplant	Tan, Brown, Gold	Blue, Green, Aqua, Teal	Leather, Silk, Pyramids, Wildlife
Bathroom	Off White, White, Beige	Rose, Red, Pink, Peach, Blush	Gray, Black, Navy, Eggplant	Tan, Brown, Gold	Blue, Green, Aqua, Teal	Animal Prints, Leather, Silk
Office or Study	Tan, Brown, Gold	Blue, Green, Aqua, Teal	Off White, White, Beige	Rose, Red, Pink, Peach, Blush	Gray, Black, Navy, Eggplant	Florals, Stripes, Linen, Cotton

When this happens it acts like a magnet drawing many other positives to it. When using Feng Shui to highlight your home, keep the chi moving gracefully can be done through the use of wonderful color. The very best way to enhance any space is by using the intention you desire for your family and the colors that you love.

Accents

We love to have all sorts of little things around us. The accent pieces we have can be anything from a chenille throw to a glorious Navajo pillow. Accessories take on more meaning if they are gathered and used according to the elements. Below is a list of some accent pieces and the elements that are associated to them. Use these in combination or alone to add accents with meaning.

Animal skin of any kind - Fire element
Clocks, radios and televisions - Metal element
Crystal vases, figurines and dishes - Water element
Decorative Pottery - Earth element
Coin collections - Metal element
Medals and trophies - Metal element
Small kitchen appliance - Metal element
Decorative lamps - Fire element
PVC Outdoor Furniture - Fire element
Wall sconces - Fire element
Wooden Picture Frames - Wood element
Baskets - Wood accents
Floral arrangements - Wood element
Etched glass - Water element
Decorative bottles - Water elements
Art tiles - Earth element
China and porcelain - Earth element
Mosaic tile - Earth element

Patterns

Patterned wallpaper, carpet, curtains, and furniture influence the nature of chi energy in a room. The effect of different patterns changes the chi because each shape is represented as one of the five elements.

The patterns used in fabrics and wall coverings are used in conjunction with an individual element.

Walls that have a mottled pattern wall covering, a faux finish such as a sponged pattern, color wash, marble, and stenciling have a water effect and are very calming. Sharply detailed wall coverings that have a sharper feeling lean toward the metal element. Stripes in wall coverings or borders represent the wood element. The planets, moon or celestial art represent earth and animals; people or characters portray the fire element.

Fabric patterns work similar to wall coverings, except they can be used on smaller items. They, too, carry with them the association of the elements.

Stars represent fire
Stripes symbolize wood
Checks depict earth
Circles represent metal
Mottled finishes represent water.

Fabrics enhance an area quickly and are cost efficient. They can be used alone, or in combination with other attributes to balance a space.

Patterns Representing Metal

Patterns in fabric or wall covering that are circular, swirling, semicircular, half moon, arched or swagged represent the metal element.

Strengthened the metal element by using earth. Too much metal in an environment causes rigidity and inability to comprise. When there is too much metal, control it with fire.

Patterns Representing Water

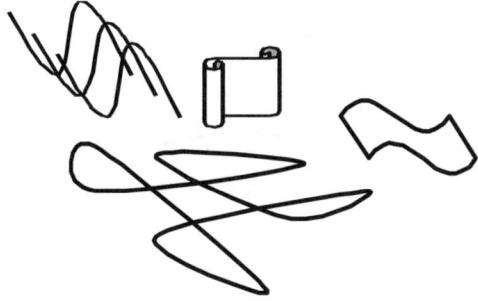

Free - flowing, snakelike, asymmetrical, curvy and wavy patterns are all related to the water element.

Strengthen by using the metal element. Too much water in an environment causes one to be passive, inconsistent and wishy-washy. When there is too much water, control it with earth.

Patterns Representing Wood

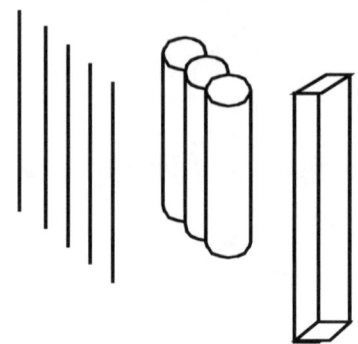

Columns, stripes, poles, beams, bands and vertical lines in patterns represent the wood element.

Strengthen by using the water element. Too much wood in an environment causes overwhelm and burnout. When there is too much wood, control it with metal.

Patterns representing fire

The patterns of triangles, sharp angels, stars and zigzags are all representations of the fire element.

Strengthen by using the wood element. When there is too much fire, control it with the water element. Too much fire in an environment causes anger and impulsive behavior.

Patterns Representing Earth

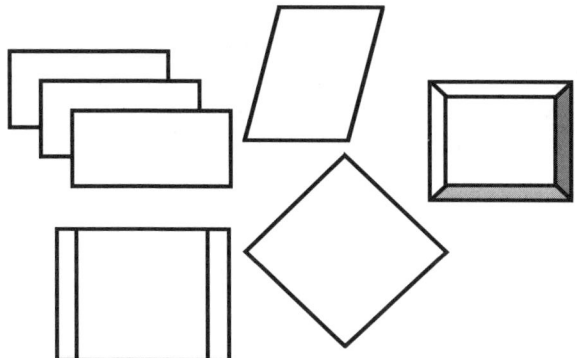

Patterns of rectangles, squares, checks, boxes and frames represent the earth element.

Strengthen by using the fire element. Too much earth in an environment causes one to be too serious and conservative. When there is too much earth, control it with wood.

Shapes and Style

Using the natural counterpart of the element can also be presented in the shape of items themselves. Where a square pattern in a fabric represents earth, so does a large rectangular picture of a beautiful hillside, because a rectangle is the shape associated to earth. Shape is the one component of an element that can be used when nothing else is possible. Since it is unobtrusive, it will fit into a decor easily.

Let's say you already have a color theme for your bedroom. You want to use peach (earth) and blue (wood). You can then add the three remaining elements by shape and style. Add fire by using a triangular throw pillow on the bed, metal with an overstuffed chair with rounded pillows and water with Queen Anne style legs on your end tables, or sheers that shimmer at the window.

Details in the construction of your house
also have an element attached to them.

A staircase with a slight curve adds the water element, which is signified by its shape without actually using water or the color black.

The style of furnishings can enhance the chi in a room. Using a high poster bed in a room with a cathedral ceiling will uplift the chi. In rooms with standard or low ceilings; low spindles or futons work best. Glass top tables invite stimulating and lively conversation, where ceramic tops on tables invite heart-to-heart talks.

Tall pieces of furniture represent growth and the wood element. These pieces include: high boys, dressers, bookcases, entertainment cabinets, grandfather clocks, and decorative trees. The stabilizing earth element is present in: low wide cabinets (such as buffets), night stands, trunks and chest of drawers. Metal and its precision is present in: round knobs on furniture, oval or circular rugs, swags, and fabrics that drape. Glass top tables, mirrors, curved legs on furnishings, and crystal accents all represent the flow of the water element. The fabrics of leather, suede, wool, silk, all lamps, and some topiary are influenced by the fire element.

Exercises:
Look up at the room you are currently in, do a quick element count. What elements are present? What is missing or weak in the room? Can anything be added to balance the room?

Program student please complete the Designing Element Work sheet Number 1206

Make your front door as welcome as possible, well-lit and easy to find.

Exercise Room

Purpose:

The workout area is a connection between body and attitude. When we feel good, life flows much better then when we don't. This is not limited to just physical it also affects the emotional.

Suggestions:

Keep the area open with plenty of room and low maintenance. Use music that is up beat and artwork that is fun. Designate this area to fitness only; it should not be a shared space.

Symbols:

Pictures of people in great shape and artwork of fruit or botanicals represent good health. Mobiles and sky art keep the chi active and helps keep the weight off.

Color:

Bright yellow is stimulates and vibrant. Crisp greens inspire freshness and blues have soothing qualities to reduce pain.

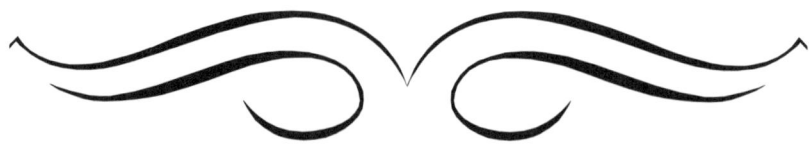

Decorating Elements

Each element is present in the shape, composition and color of an item. Every time you bring an item to your home you are adding an additional element as well.

When the elements are balanced in the decor of your home you create a serene and healthy space.

When first beginning to work with the elements being aware of where a decorating accessory fits on the elemental chart makes the choice easier. At those times we need to fix, add or redo to our home knowing what to look for can save time and money. Looking for the right item one that also enhances the elements in a room adds to the good health of all that live there.

Every item represents an element. Though color will introduce an element to a space, it is best to know what an item is made of to further enhance the decor of a room. When you know all the elemental aspects of an item it is easier to know the best location for the item in your home.

Floors

The floors in our home represent the foundation in which we walk. We obtain access to each room in our house by following the direction laid out by the flooring. Everyone that enters your space, including pets, use the floor to move through the house. What the floor does is; create the pathway for the chi of move and to connect each section of the space into one unit, our home.

Floorings that support wood are:
Wood planks, wood squares, and parquet.
Floorings that support fire are:
Wool carpet, and sisal
Floorings that support earth are:
Ceramic tile, mosaic, brick, adobe, and rectangular rugs
Floorings that support metal are:
Granite, marble stone, round or oval rugs, and Berber carpet
Floorings that support water are:
High-gloss Floor Paints and shiny surfaces

Walls

The dictionary defines walls as the fortification of a structure. In Feng Shui the walls represent the strength and reinforcement of a family. Over the years walls in our homes have transformed from merely dividers to decorative marvels. Walls have become backdrops to art and used as photo galleries. They are decorative accents when painted and wallpapered, and add dimension to a space.

Wall covering supporting wood is:
Stripes, florals, verticals, leaf patterns, and paneling
Wall covering supporting fire is:
Characters with the sun, moon, people or animals

Wall covering supporting earth is: Stucco, textured paint, rag rolling
Wall covering supporting metal is:
Sponge painting, marbling, and faux finishes
Wall covering supporting water is:
Foil paper, Moiré, and watermarks

Fabrics and textiles

In western homes we use a range of different textiles adding interest and individual personality to the places we spend time. Everything from our dish towels to the mattress cover is made of an element and can be used to further strengthen the overall balance of a room.

Fabrics supporting wood are:
Cotton, linen, burlap, jute
Fabrics supporting fire are:
Wool, silk, suede, leather, fur and mohair
Fabrics supporting earth are:
African mud clothe
Fabrics supporting metal are:
Aluminum, brass, chrome, and stainless steel
Fabrics supporting water are:
Moiré, Mylar, angel hair, and crystal

Window treatments

Covering up our windows, at least in the private areas of our homes, is a practice that most of us use. Over the years our window treatments have become not just practical, but beautiful additions to our homes. Since these items have become such an important part of decorating our homes, the element that certain styles represent will help to balance the space we live in.

Window treatments supporting wood are:
Verticals, wood blinds, shutters, and shades
Window treatments supporting fire are:
PVC blinds, plastic and resin blinds
Window treatments supporting earth are:
Drapery panels, tab top curtains
Window treatments supporting metal are:
Poufs, balloon shades, swags, aluminum blinds
Window treatments supporting water are:
Mylar solar shades, sheers, fiberglass draperies

Furniture styles

The purpose of furniture is to support us by making us comfortable. Since the type of furniture is so persona, l keeping certain styles in mind when you need a new item is easy to do when you know what element a room needs and what is depicted by that element.

When all the elements are present it is nice to add more of a particular element that will draw the chi of opportunity to a situation. For example if you want to keep life prosperous in every way, after the room is balanced add a little more fire and wood. The fire will ignite the chi of fortunate blessings while the wood will help them grow.

Furniture pieces supporting wood are:
Highboys, grandfather clock, entertainment cabinet
Furniture pieces supporting fire are:
Laminate, particleboard, plastic, and resin
Furniture pieces supporting earth are:
Low squatty chests, trunks, night stands

Furniture pieces supporting metal are:
Over-stuffed cushions, padded arms, throw pillows, and tassels
Furniture pieces supporting water are:
Mirrors, glass, acrylic, Queen Anne and Georgian styles

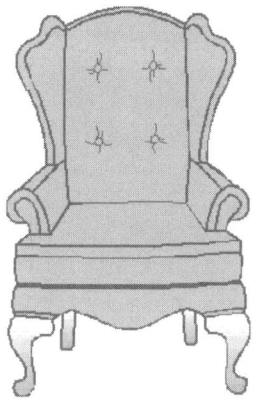

This Queen Anne chair represents the water element because
of the curve of the winged back and the legs.

Accessories

Each item in our homes should tell a story about the people
that live there. Every object has its own chi and is alive with the
memories and associations we attach to them. Since our homes
reflect who we really are, then wisely selecting accents that we truly
love becomes a sure way to surround ourselves with love. When
we bring in all five elements joyfully into a space those same elements act as personal affirmations.

Accessory styles supporting wood are:
Beams, columns, poles, plant stands and flowers
Accessory styles supporting fire are:
Candles, fireplaces, lighting, fireplaces, and lamps

Accessory styles supporting earth are:
Square picture frames, porcelain, pottery and china
Accessory styles supporting metal are:
Iron, steel, tin, aluminum, gold, silver, and pewter
Accessory styles supporting water are:
Crystal, snow globes, mirrors, ice sculptures and glass

Shape

Shapes are a vital key to adding an element when color, style or pattern isn't appropriate. Look around the room you are currently sitting in. The different shapes are what make a house a home. Different elemental shapes add depth and interest to rooms. Pay attention to the items you love, notice the shape and how it makes you feel; joyful, happy, or meditative. Chances are that shape is what your soul needs to feel peaceful. Shapes have a separate form of chi attached to them further strengthening the harmony of the house.

Shapes that support wood are:
Columnar and Vertical
Shapes that support fire are:
Triangle, Pyramid, and Cone
Shapes that support earth are:
Square and Rectangle
Shapes that support metal are:
Circular, Oval, and Octagon
Shapes that support water are:
Asymmetrical, Curved, and Free-forms

Making beautiful, healthy choices

In "every day" decorating choices, it can be challenging to decide how to implement an element into your decor. When you need an item like flooring or window treatments, it is helpful to know not only how to purchase an item but which element it will represent.

Let's say you need a new chair and the room needs the earth element.

First: Look at what <u>element</u> nourishes earth. According to the nourishing cycle, it is fire. The two elements are earth and fire. Earth is the element weak in the room, and fire because it nourishes or creates earth.

Second: Look at the <u>colors</u> associated to earth. These are yellow, orange, brown and earth tones. Okay, lets say you like those tones and they will work with your decor. But what if you didn't like them? Since fire is the element that supports earth. You would then explore some of the red tones representing fire.

Third: Look at the <u>fabrics</u> associated to earth. No help there because African mud cloth is not that easy to find for chair fabric. So look at the fabric choices associated with fire: leather, silk, wool.

Fourth: The <u>style</u> of the chair needs to be squatty or square, with short legs to represent earth. The pattern of the fabric could be textured to further strengthen earth.

What kind of chair will you look for? A chair with short legs that is slightly over stuffed to look squatty (symbolizing earth), covered in either a wool blend or leather in tan, gold, persimmon, or the red family (adding nourishing fire.)

Decorating Element Chart

ITEM	WOOD	FIRE	EARTH	METAL	WATER
Flooring	wood planks, wood squares, parquet	wool carpet, sisal	ceramic tile, mosaic, brick, adobe, rectangular rugs	granite, marble, stone, round or oval rugs	high gloss floor paints
Wall Covering and Patterns	stripes, florals, leaf patterns, paneling	characters with the sun or moon, people, animals	stucco, textured paint, rag rolling	sponge painting, marble painting, cloud painting	foil papers, moiré, watermarks, mirrors
Fabrics and Materials	cotton, linen, burlap, jute	wool, silk, suede, leather, fur	African mud cloth	aluminum, brass, iron chrome, stainless steel	moiré, Mylar, glass, crystal
Window Treatments	vertical blinds, wood blinds, pleated and Roman shades	pvc blinds, plastic blinds	drapery panels, tab top curtains	poufs balloon shades, swags, aluminum blinds	Mylar solar shades, sheers
Furnishings	high boys, grandfather clocks, entertainment cabinets	laminate, plastic, resin	low "squatty" chests, trunks, night stands	over-stuffed cushions, padded arms, throw pillows, tassels	mirrors, glass, clear acrylic, Queen Ann, Georgian,
Accessories	beams, columns, ploes	candles, fireplaces, lighting fixtures	square picture frames, porcelain, china	iron, steel, tin, aluminum, gold, silver,, pewter	crystal, snow globes, glass paperweights
Shape	columnar, and vertical	triangle, pyramid, and cone	square and rectangle	circle, oval, and octagon	asymmetrical, curved, and freeform

Decorating Element Chart

When faced with the uncertainty of how to bring in the elements through a decorative touch, refer to the *Decorating Element Chart* and your choices will be clearer. This is only a guideline. With all the products on the market, it is virtually impossible to list all the items that are elementally available.

Using the Decorating Element Chart

Look around the room you will be working on and notice how the elements are currently represented there. Such as, the lamp that is a fire symbol or the mirror representing water. List the decorative pieces you want to replace or add, like purchasing new curtains or adding a side chair. Take note of the elements present or elements that are missing or weak. Match the element you need with the decorative item you want on the Decorating Element chart. Then the only thing left to do is -- go shopping!

Exercise:
Is there one thing in particular that you long to have in your life? What symbol could you attach to it to give the Universe a clear message of what it is? What quality best supports the desire?

Program students please complete the Decorating Elements Work sheet Number 1207

Wisdoms

Laundry Room

Purpose:

The laundry room is symbolic of renewal and freshness. Many times this area is used as a second foyer inviting us home after a long day at work.

Suggestions:

This area should be inviting and fun. Use things that make you feel wonderful each time you see it. Keep the area well organized with supplies behind closed doors.

Symbols:

Hang children's art or fun wallpaper. Create a gallery of family portraits or seascapes to remind you of the beach. Or hang travel posters that in courage you to dream of exotic places.

Color:

Primary red and yellow wake up the senses. Magenta and turquoise stir the soul. While peach, rose and sage green evoke a feeling of peace and home.

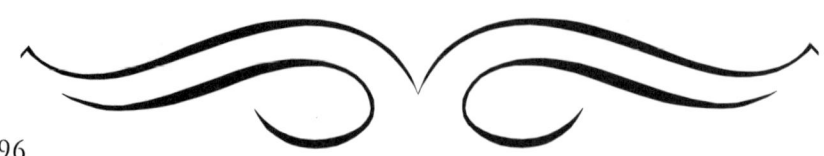

Types of
Chi Energy

Just as each element has a list of characteristics, each has a type of energy connected to it as well. The wood element has a nourishing, healthy type of chi perfect for family rooms, kitchens, exercise rooms or baths. The fire element is a very social energy-one of action, getting up and getting started. This works well in the bedrooms, dens, meeting areas and dining rooms. Earth energies are very stable; they are reflected best in halls, staircases, laundry rooms or central gathering areas. Metal energies are sharp and evoke being on the cutting edge and innovative ideas; they are great for home offices, studios, craft areas or writing desks. The energy that is present in water is one of freedom, flowing free, and easy transitions. Great areas of the home for the water element are front entries, living rooms, the garage, and great rooms.

**Often it is necessary
that we change the chi which is present in a room.**

Since we don't always have the luxury of changing the location of a room, there are times when you will want to change the chi present there.

For example, a child's room that is represented by the fire element will not support your child if they are not feeling well. To encourage healthy and nourishing chi, adding the wood element is the best representation.

Jacksonville Judy

Before Judy had eye surgery she wanted the universal chi energies to support her recovery. Her bedroom was in the back of the house and done in pink and white. Though these colors supported her intention of finding a mate, they did nothing to aid in a speedy comeback. She changed the sheets to green (health) and yellow (balance). She added a small silk tree to denote growing health and added a water fountain for ease in feeling great. Since she would not be able to see well, hearing the water would give her a sense of peace. Judy healed in half the time predicted and believes that is was because of her good Feng Shui practices.

Bring in the element

It isn't always necessary to add an element to a room in order to change the type of chi. Sometimes just removing an element that is present there will do the trick. If you are feeling stuck or unmovable in life, chances are there may be too much of the earth element or earth chi present. Begin by taking away the element that is dominating; in this case it's earth. When it isn't possible to remove an element, then refer to the controlling cycle and add the controlling element to govern the chi that is present there. When you are feeling stuck, add plants or flowers to your living room or bedroom.

Controlling Cycle:

Wood consumes Earth
Earth dams Water
Water extinguishes Fire
Fire melts Metal
Metal cuts Wood

Each element carries a wonderful chi quality attached to it. When they are healthy and balanced, the chi that is present will aid you in creating a well-balanced and harmonious life-style.

When in balance, the wood element denotes: intuition, flexibility, cooperation, and trust. Progressive in thought, open to expansion and new thinking relates to this chi.

When in balance, the fire element denotes: leadership, excitement, vitality and assertiveness. Setting trends and making things happen is the association here.

When in balance, the earth element denotes: stability, practical, physical, and grounding. Being organized is connected to this chi.

When in balance, the metal element denotes: wit, concentration, brilliance, determination, and stamina. Clarity of mind is the association.

When in balance, the water element denotes: relaxation, meditation, mystical, calming, and flow. A deeper connection to spirituality is the chi attached to this element.

Removing the Element

The type of chi present in a room also affects emotions you are feeling. To change the chi in a room, simply change the element. Use the element connected to the emotion you want to eliminate.

If you are feeling:

Unable to grow or lack trust
Add the wood element, such as: flowers, trees, or a wooden table.

Low, depressed, lack of excitement or unmotivated
Add the fire element, such as: candles, brighter bulbs, or a laminated table.

Spacey, disconnected or separated from the world
Add the earth element, such as: earthenware pottery, or a ceramic top table.

Weak, indecisive or wishy washy
Add the metal element, such as: brass vase, pewter pot, or a wrought iron table.

Stressed, anxious or tearful
Add the water element, such as: crystal vase, snow globe, or a glass top table

Tip:

Purple is the color that enhances wealth, and the number four and birds support prosperity. Use four purple birds in the wealth area of your home is said to bring good fortune.

The Elements   Type of Chi

WOOD — growing, nuorishing, wholesome, beginnings

FIRE — action, activity, motivation, vibration

EARTH — stability, security, grounding, balance

METAL — sharp, detailed, serious, progressive, precise

WATER — clarity, effortless flow, emotioal, sensitive

The above are only suggestions. Refer back to
Chapter 5 Reflecting Earth for more on the elements
and their associations.

The Mastery of Chi

The ability to change the chi present in an area is a masterful way to change the events around you. Though chi has a wonderful effect on your surroundings, equally important is the effect it has on your body. Knowing which part of the body is strengthened or weakened by an element enables you to balance them when you need to.

Wood affects the liver, gall bladder, and blood. Pressure points are in the feet an toes.
Example: When working on issues of nourishment or growth wear a green belt shirt, or green socks.

Fire affects the heart, bones and small intestine. Pressure points are located in the hand and wrist.
Example: When you are in need of action, wear a red blouse, long scarf, red kerchief in you pocket, or wear a ruby or red garnet ring.

Earth affects the spleen, pancreas, and stomach. Pressure points in the knee and leg.
Example: When feeling detached or alone, wear yellow or earth tone shorts, pajamas, slacks or brown socks covering the calves.

Metal affects lungs, colon, and head. Pressure points are in the collarbone and ribs.
Example: When trying out new ideas for the first time, wear a light colored scarf, earrings, turtleneck or tie.

Water affects kidneys, bladder and reproduction system. Pressure points in the sole of the foot and ankle.
Example: When you need to change direction in your life, wear black, navy or charcoal undergarments, shorts, slacks, or shoes.

It's Elemental, My Dear

It is hard for most people to consider the elements without seeing the room. Color plays such an important role in our life, that a black and white world seems oddly disoriented. However, it is crucial to be able to pick out the elements by their shape and content as well as by their color.

Another reason for being able to locate the elements in your home is to bring your vital chi back to nature; it has little to do with how well you can decorate. Feng Shui should be used to create sacred spaces; not as an interior decorating trick. There is nothing wrong with mixing the concept of design and Feng Shui, but they are separate tools; one being creative, the other being healing.

Regardless whether you use them together or separately, the concept of nature is the one truth. We all need to feel that connection, even if it is just in a photo. Feng Shui is a marriage of many concepts, all relating to the inner peace that each of us seek.

Don't get caught up in the way your space looks. Pay attention first to how it feels, then add the beauty with things that you love and desire. Consciously use items that represent how the elements in your space connect you to a greater power; one that forms the universal chi to aide us in our life journey, and that alone is a thing of beauty.

Exercise

Which element dominates your living room? Your bedroom and your kitchen? What can you use to control it?

Program students please complete the Type of Chi Work sheet Number 1208

To become a Program student refer to the *Feng Shui Tutor Program* in the back of this book

Section III

Wisdoms

Kitchen

Purpose:

The kitchen is where we prepare our food, read the mail, check homework, write letters, and chat with friends. It is the galley the hub of the home, a multifaceted jewel that supports health, prosperity and wholesomeness.

Suggestions:

Keep counters clutter free. While working at the stove, be sure that the door is visible to the cook. Door to the kitchen should open freely. Use good lighting here.

Symbols:

Bowls of fresh fruit represent strength. Wooden bowls and spoons denote growth. Using a good working stove represents wealth. Ceramic tile symbolizes foundation.

Color:

Yellow stimulates joy. Shades of orange like peach or salmon spark conversation and brown and taupe add balance.

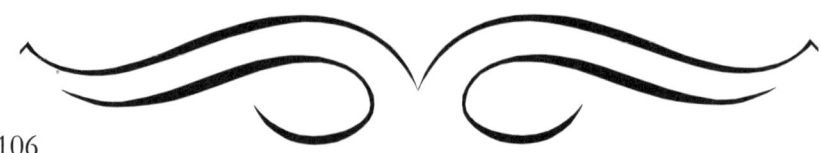

Qualities
and the Bagua

In addition to applying practical methods to enhance one's life, the chi energy can be improved in your home through the application of a Feng Shui development called the Bagua. When used in connection to the "Qualities" this powerful tool influences everyday life in a practical way. The Bagua is a map of the Qualities of Life that are divided into sections of life situations — career, helpful people, children, love, fame, wealth, family, knowledge and center. In Feng Shui, the Bagua is superimposed on rooms, buildings and plots of land to resolve problems or to manifest dreams.

By locating a particular quality that you want to work on in your home, you are given the added benefit of drawing positive chi to that area.

**Each quality or situation is assigned a specific location
in your home and is found on the Bagua.**

Life's Qualities

Career and Direction
Helpful People
Children and Creativity
Love and Marriage
Fame and Reputation
Wealth and Riches
Family and Health
Knowledge and Spirituality
Center —Yin/Yang

Living Life

Life comes complete with ups and downs.

Unexpected situations can cause our money to deplete, a loved one could get sick or marriage mishaps can happen. The Chinese believe that an understanding of the Bagua, the Qualities of Life, and how they relate to our homes, bodies and fortune allows us to manipulate, even change, our fate.

When the Bagua is used to reinforce conditions in your life the results explode with healthy chi energy and attract many positive changes. The Bagua produces successful results when two forces are used in combination; the wisdom of how to use the tool and a serious intention to change your life.

The Basics

The Bagua Map is a Chinese table used to locate the "Qualities of Life in your space. The original Bagua was based on the nine magic squares of the _I Ching the Chinese Book of Changes._ According to the ancient Feng Shui teaching, each section of the Bagua is called a gua. This is a 3000-year-old philosophy that predates Taoism and Confucianism.

BAGUA BASICS

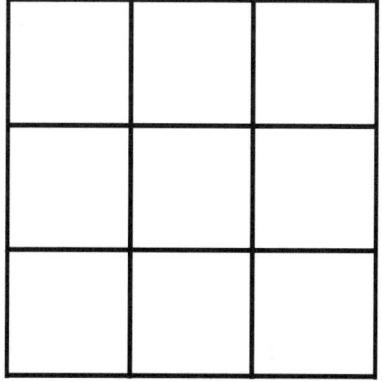

The Bagua map is divided into nine squares. Each square is represented by a "Quality of Life"

A quality or life situation is assigned to each gua and doesn't change. The map is then superimposed on a plot of land, a home, a room, and even flat surfaces like a desk or table.

Before the Bagua can be placed on any area, the qualities must first be assigned to a particular section or gua.

To start this labeling process of assigning a quality to the map, first divide the qualities into two groups. These are distinguished as either cardinal or supporting locations. The cardinal locations are those areas that maintain an anchored position on the Bagua while the supporting locations are the corner guas.

Cardinal Locations (guas)
Career
Family and Health
Children and Creativity
Fame and Reputation
Yin/ Yang

Cardinal guas have individual attributes associated with them and supporting guas are combination areas.

CARDINAL LOCATIONS

	Fame and Reputation	
Family and Health	Yin / Yang	Children and Ceativity
	Career and Journey	

The supporting guas are comprised of two primary locations. This is a combination of itself and the two neighboring cardinal locations.

Supporting Locations (guas)
       Helpful People & Travel
       Love & Marriage
       Wealth & Abundance
       Knowledge & Spirituality

SUPPORTING LOCATIONS

Wealth and Abundance		**Love and Marriage**
Knowledge and Spituality		**Helpful People and Travel**

Both type of qualities and locations are equally important and all "Qualities" have a major affect on our life. Be cautious not to trivialize any of them just because you may not need them at the time. When balancing spaces, all locations are secured equally.

Using the "Qualities" with location

The nine squares of the Bagua are linked together in a table. In other styles of Feng Shui you will see the Bagua in the shape of an octagon instead of a rectangle. All we have done is squared the edges, making it easier to apply to a floor plan. We now apply the "Quality" to the coordinating location or section of the Bagua.

When all the qualities are applied to the Bagua the completed map has all locations permanently filled and they never change. This tool shows us exactly where to concentrate when a life situation happens, you can literally look at the Bagua to see what qualities applies. However, rarely does a situation occur that affects only one "Quality". To further strengthen the chi energy around a given situation, it may be necessary to add a second quality to balance.

Completed Bagua Map

When a situation is attached to a location, it is always best to create a balance of the qualities. Simply attaching the situation to a second quality will do this. When you counter balance with another quality, the chi not only is stronger but more stable.

A Situation

Sally is trying to complete her degree in anthropology. In order to finish her thesis she needs to interview a well know authority on the subject of "Past and Fallen Kings". However, the only person she knows of is a professor working in Cairo, Egypt.

Let's look at the above situation. The primary Quality of Life would be knowledge and spirituality for a couple reasons. Sally is trying to finish her degree <u>and</u> through an interview she would gain more knowledge.

So what would be the second or balancing quality? It could be fame because she would gain notoriety for her work, or love and marriage from building strong, work relations with the professor. Career is possible because it is her adventure in life, her passion

Choosing helpful people and travel would be a good balancing quality. The reason being that perhaps she could find another authority (helpful person) that was closer to her, or a way to travel to Egypt. Either way, the single gua of helpful people and travel would balance both needs.

Sometimes it can be difficult to judge what would be the best supporting Quality of Life. In those cases I have found that the best thing to do is to follow your instincts. Pick the one that means the most to you.

COMPLETED BAGUA MAP

Wealth and Abudance	Fame and Reputation	Love and Marriage
Health and Family	Yin / Yang	Children and Creativity
Knowledge and Spirituality	Career and Journey	Helpful People and Travel

Applying the Proper Quality of Life

Finding how the qualities are associated to situations in our life and locating those on the Bagua are only part of the process to support our life through Feng Shui. The next step is to learn how to apply these principals to our home. The Chinese believe that our homes mirror what is going on in our life. Following this belief, we begin to look at our homes as not just places to live but a sacred space to rejuvenate and magnify great things in our life. There are specific times when you should scrutinize your home to be sure that they support your desires.

1. When the same negative situation keeps reoccurring.
2. To get the chi to support a desire or dream
3. When fear creeps up on you.
4. To ensure life is in balance.
5. When you are brokenhearted.

When the same negative situation keeps reoccurring.

Matthew seems to have problems drawing healthy relationships to himself. Over the past fifteen years he has been in six long-term relationships. Due to conflicts at work, he has been transferred to several different departments and he has had no contact with his personal family in three years.

To support Matthew we would look at the relationship area of his home and knowledge and spirituality to find out what inside him he is mirroring.

Allowing the chi to support a desire, dream or need.

Bev loves the beach. Her dream is to have a home near the water so she can walk and meditate on the sands whenever she wants to. To bring her dream into reality she visualizes herself at the seaside daily. She has a picture of a beautiful surf-side home and started a "cottage" fund putting back ten dollars a week. Finally, every vacation she can is spent on or near the water.

To support Bev we would concentrate on the wealth and abundance gua and to further balance her dream, helpful people and travel.

When fear creeps up on you.

Thomas has a wonderful home he shares with his life partner. A great job, supporting family and financial security are all gifts he enjoys. Two years ago a small tumor was removed from his lung and recent tests show another spot on the same lung.

Two areas we would concentrate on for Thomas are health and family to strengthen fitness, and prevention. Learning about what causes us fear gives us back the control to better understand how to deal with threatening situations. This would direct us to take a look at the knowledge and spirituality area.

To ensure that life is in balance

Kerstin has three great children. They live in a safe neighborhood in a beautiful home and her husband has a job that affords for her to stay at home with the children. Relationships are good within the immediate family as well as the extended family. Everyone is healthy and life is good to them.

115

The primary location to check out in the home would be center or yin/yang to further add strength and the balancing would, of course, be family. Giving your home a Feng Shui safety check is a good idea to spot potential problems before they happen.

When you are broken hearted.

Treva worked hard at her job for twenty-five years. She received many awards for her outstanding record and was voted employee of the year, three years in a row. One day without warning, the company closed its doors; leaving Treva and 200 other workers without jobs. Fast approaching the age of sixty she is devastated.

The area of attention here would be helpful people. Right now she could use some help sorting out her options. Next, concentrate on career to help give her a sense of direction.

By using the Bagua to locate the quality that you desire, you can literally use rooms in your homes to reflect the positives you want to happen in your life. This process starts with three easy steps.

1. Identify which "Quality of Life" is needed to support your dream.
2. Locate the area of your home that relates to the quality.
3. Symbolically reflect your dream in that area.

Keep the desire clear, choose a cardinal location on the Bagua and a quality to balance it, this opens the pathways for the chi energies to flow freely. To better understand the flow of this energy take a close look at what your home is trying to tell you about your life. The Bagua is a tool that helps you identify, raise and change the chi quickly to keep life running smoothly.

Exercise:

Pick a situation in your life or a firneds life. Which cardianl and supporting Qualitiy of Life would apply.

Program students please complete Qualities and the Bagua Work sheet Number 1309

Wisdoms

Bathroom

Purpose:

The bathroom is symbolic of flowing water and flowing finances (money). Discover the wealth that hides in those walls. They are your sanctuary, spa, and meditation cove; and should be treated with luxury.

Suggestions:

Keep toilet and bathroom doors closed. Avoid having the toilet in clear view from the door. Always keep the bath smelling sweet and clean.

Symbols:

Accessories that shine like brass or crystal keep the chi moving at a lively pace. Use plants in clay pots to represent steady, financial growth.

Color:

Purple and red support financial wealth. Rose suggests blossoming and sage green denotes the development of wisdom.

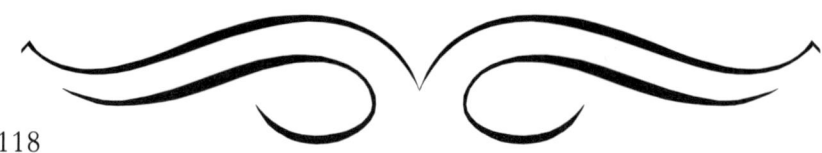

The Elements and the Bagua

Understanding how each element affects us individually teaches us how to best use them. The elements not only balance a space but also can change the direction in which the chi moves. This is particularly helpful when responding to life situations.

The Qualities of Life correspond with life situations and are of benefit when working in a particular area. The elements are tools that purify an area. The elements also correspond to a cardinal location or quality. When used in combination, the earth chi becomes more solid and brings about positive chi flow.

You may add the earth element to any or all the "qualities" to stabilize them. Earth is like placing a foot firmly on the ground; planting yourself and readying for the long duration. It is being steadfast, steady, confident and sure. Adding it to a supporting location, or any location for that matter, will create a secure, even pace of chi.

Working with the types of chi

The true essence of Feng Shui is chi. Every time you use Feng Shui principals in your life the reason behind the action is to get the chi to move towards a positive, to better our lives.

Knowing what type of chi is drawn by an element and a quality better prepares us on how to use this aspect is our life.

Cardinal Locations

Water and effortless flow suggests Career and Direction.

Children and Creativity is progressive and always moving ahead, it is detailed and sharp like a tack (metal).

Fame and Reputation is sparked (fire) by action and motivation.

Family and Health is represented by growth and nurturing chi, which is present in wood.

The center, the yin and yang, balances all the areas through grounding and stability. It is the land (earth) we walk on.

Both the element and the quality are used either in conjunction or as a substitute for each other. The element and the type of chi attached to it fits into the Bagua in the same location as the Quality of Life. If the element is given the quality can be assumed, because the element symbolizes the type of chi present.

Cardinal Location	Element	Color	Type of Chi
Career	Water	Black, Dark Tones	Effortless flow
Children and Creativity	Metal	White, Pastels	Details and New ideas
Fame and Reputation	Fire	Red	Action and Motivation
Family and Health	Wood	Green, Blue	Nurturing and Growth
Yin/Yang	Earth	Yellow, Earth tones	Grounding and Stability

Lower center area (gua)

Career and Direction is associated with water. The type of chi denotes flow, and fulfillment. The color attached to this area is black, navy blue, and dark tones.

Center right hand area (gua)

The Children and Creativity attracts the metal element. This chi is detailed, sharp and precise. The color attached to this area is white, off whites and pastels.

CARDINAL LOCATIONS WITH ELEMENTS CHI
AND COLOR

	Fame and Reputation *Fire-Red* Action, Motivation	
Health and Family *Wood-Green/Blue* Nurturing, Growth	**Yin/Yang** *Earth-Yellow Tones* Grounding, Stable	**Children and Creativity** *Metal-White, Pastels* New Ideas
	Career *Water-Black, Dark Tones* Effortless Flow	

Upper Center area (gua)

Fame and Reputation is best associated to the fire element. It denotes being social, fast paced and motivated. Colors are shades of red, pink, peach and burgundy

Center left hand area (gua)

Family and Health is associated to the nurturing element of
wood. It denotes upward growth, new beginnings, wholeness
and The colors are blue and green.

Center area (gua)

Yin and Yang, the core is associated to the stabling element
of earth. It denotes foundation, fortitude and grounding. The
color connection here is earth tones, brown and yellow.

Supporting Locations

The secondary or supporting location are located on the corner areas of the Bagua. These Qualities of Life are combination
guas, because they take on the attributes of the Quality and the
element on either side of the Bagua. This gives the secondary guas
an assigned quality, and borrows all the characteristics of the connecting areas

Helpful People and Travel is supported by water and metal
represents calm and precise.
Love and Marriage is supported by metal and fire represents
social and detailed.
Wealth and Abundance is supported by fire and wood represents a fast upward growth.
Knowledge and Spirituality is supported by wood and water
represents contemplation and serenity.

Supporting Location	Element	Color	Type of Chi
Helpful People and Travel	Water/ Metal	Grey	Calm precision
Love and Marriage	Fire/ Metal	Pink	Creative motivation
Wealth and Abundance	Fire/ Wood	Purple	Active growth
Knowledge and Spirituality	Wood/ Water	Teal	Contemplative stillness

Lower right hand area (gua)

Helpful People and Travel. It draws the calm water from Career and the precise metal energy from Children and Creativity. The color attached to this area would be gray. (Combining black and white).

Upper right hand area (gua)

The Love and Marriage sector of the Bagua has the attached elements of both motivating fire from Fame and Reputation, and sharp metal from Children and Creativity. The color attached to this area is pink. (Combining red and white).

SUPPORTING LOCATIONS WITH ELEMENTS CHI AND COLOR

Wealth and Abundance *Fire/Wood* *Purple* Active growth		**Love and Marriage** *Fire/Metal* *Pink* Creative motivation
Knowledge and Spirituality *Wood/Water* *Teal* Contemplative stillness		**Helpful People and Travel** *Water/Metal* *Gray* Calm precision

Lower left hand area (gua)

In the Knowledge and Spirituality area we combine the inner growth of contemplation related to the wood element and Family and Health with the still water for Career. The color is teal. (Combining black and green).

Upper left hand area (gua)

Lastly, the gua we label Wealth and Abundance integrates the rapid fire of Fame and Reputation and the upward growth of wood and Family and Health. The color is purple (Combining both red and blue).

Combining the Elements

Each of the nine Qualities of Life now has not only an element and a type of chi energy attached to them. They also have all the attributes, and associations of both the Quality of Life and the natural element, such as color, shape, direction, animal and etc. Using a Quality of Life, an element, or any association by itself is a powerful tool. But using them together is dynamic. These attributes, when used in combination, give us a variety of items to use when balancing a space. We are no longer just directed by color or style, but now can associate the type of chi to an actual situation in our life. Let's say that you really don't like your job and you want a new one.

The first thing we recognize is that:
you don't like your job.

This alone can affect many aspects of your life: maybe you're not sleeping (Health and Family), or are irritable with your spouse (Love and Marriage). What you do in that case is to check the chi energy in those areas first. If you're not sleeping, you would definitely want to make sure that symbols of rest and serenity were in clear view so that you could see them before you went to bed each night. The elements that are calming, nurturing, and serene are wood and water.

Examples of rest and serenity: Green sheets, a picture of the woods, striped pajamas. Some decorative items are: plants, a painting of an old wooden barn. It's interesting that wood is connected to Health and Family while water is connected to Career.

This brings us to our second point:

you want a new career.

Career is associated to the effortless flow of our life adventure. The key words are effortless, unrestricted - with no physical help or prodding from us. Water is the element.

Now, STOP — THINK — What is it that you would want the water to do? Flow down or up? Do you want it to rush or to meander? Chances are you would want it to flow up, perhaps to rush at first (so that you find the job quicker), and then to flow in a pattern of ease.

> Symbols of career flowing up: Photos of fountains with a jutting spray and colored lights. Or a mirror with a black frame hung high on the wall. Later you could change these to a reflective pool or artwork of freshly fallen snow.

Elementally combining all the characteristics

When the Quality of Life, the elements, and all attributes are combined, we add dimension to the Bagua.

> For example when locating the section of Fame and Reputation on the Bagua; the color red, number nine, season of summer, rubies, wool, animals, etc., also relate to that section of the gua.

The tools we now have available to us for adjusting the chi in our homes becomes full of possibilities. By adding our own personal symbols we create a combination that will draw powerful chi and produce dynamic results that daily mirror positive flow through our life situations.

The Dimensional Map

The Qualities of Life mirror situations that are happening, or that we desire to happen in our lives. The elements are powerful chi activators. They can be used alone to strengthen and balance any area or used in conjunction with the quality to add a secure foundation. Any attribute of either the quality or the element can also be used alone or in partnership with each other. This adds a powerful dimension to the blueprint or map, and to how to apply them to our homes, offices, and even hotel rooms.

**By this time is becomes apparent that the
Bagua is multifaceted.**

What started out to be the map of "The Qualities of Life" has grown to encompass all the aspects of both, the "Quality of Life and the elements. This complete reference tool is how the quantity of chi is intensified, reinforcing your home -- not just by one symbol but by having access to a multitude of ways to balance and enhance any area. Using the characteristics together doubles their effect, creating layers of stable chi.

A Reference Bagua Map is one that lists as many attributes as possible on it and includes your own personal symbols, things that are near and dear to you. The completed Bagua on the next page has many suggestions but it will not be complete without the addition of your symbols, ones that best suit your needs.

Exercise

Choose an area of life that you want to improve. Once you've decided on the best cardinal and supporting locations place a personal symbol made of the appropriate element. Record anything out of the ordinary that happens in the next thirty days.

Program students please complete the Working with the Energy Work sheet Number 1310

Reference Bagua Map

Wealth and Abundance	Fame and Reputation	Love and Marriage
Fire/Wood Active growth	Fire Action and Motivation	Fire/Metal Creative motivation
Purple, four, hip/bone, symbols of both Fame and Reputation combined with Family and Health, red, blue, green , triangles pyramids, columns, birds, animals, silk, wool, gold, silver, money and gifts from affluent people.	Birds, nine, summeer and eyes, red, burgundy,raisin, triangles pyramids, lights, candles, fireplaces., awards trophies anmilas, people, mohair, wool, silk, leather.. The Sun	Pink, two, organs,. symbols of both Fame and Reputation combined with Children and Creativity, red, white, pastels, peach, triangles, cones circles and ovals, pictures of couples, heart, stones, marble and granite.
Family and Health	**Yin/ Yan, Center, and Core**	**Children and Creativity**
Wood Nurturing and Growth	Earth Stable foundation	Metal Details and New ideas
Dragon,three, feet, seven, green, blue, flowers, plants, fruit, columns, beams, stripes, poles, linen, cotton, anything made of wood, art of sports figurse, friends and family. The Tree	Connetcts the other eight guas together, five, back , spinal column, yellow, brown, earth tones, rectangles, squares, globes, desert, sandy beaches, items made of earthen ware, ceramic, concrete, clay and resin The Soil	Tigar, seven, autumn and mouth, white, pastels, circles, arch ,ovals, granite marble, natural stoens, gems, crafts, artwork, wrought iron, brass, coins, whimsical items, toys, pictures of children or children's art.. The Mountain
Knowledge and Spirituality	**Career, Direction and Journey**	**Helpful People and Travel**
Wood/Water Contmplative stillness	Water Effortless flow	Metal/Water Calm precision
Teal, eight, hands, symbols of both Career combined with and Family and Health,tourquoise,teal, agua, black, navy blue, books, magazines, libraries, learning centers, free forms, winding, columns, poles and stripes.	Tortoise, one, winter and ears, black, navy blue and dark tones, free flowing, asymmetricals, mirrors, water features, artwork depicting water, aquariums, crystals, mylar foil and glass. The Sea	Gray, six, head, symbols of both Children and Creativity combined with Career.,black, white, free flowing, circles and ovals, asymmetricals, travel momentos, maps, water features, and photos of teachers.

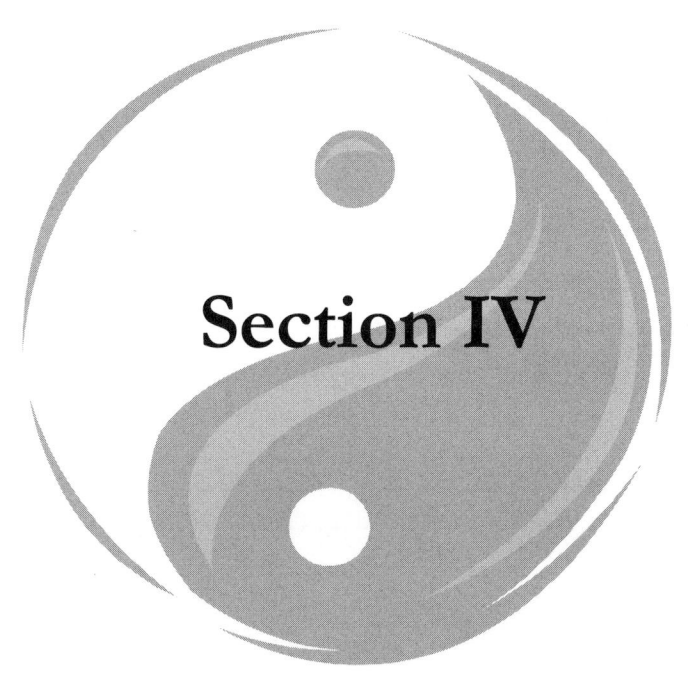

Section IV

Home Office

Purpose:

The home office is where your creativity and success originates. It is where you connect to an outside source, treat it as you would a prized possession.

Suggestions:

Offices are best housed in the front of the home. Sit so that you have a clear view of the door. Being well organized and neat is a must.

Symbols:

Circular furniture represents harmony with clients. Tie a red ribbon on the telephone cord to help draw in more clients and hanging a faceted crystal over the phone will help it ring more.

Color:

Offices that are detailed use whites and pastels
Red work great for fast paced businesses. Use green and blue for health professionals. Black , navy blue or charcoal gray are best saved for the entertainment field.

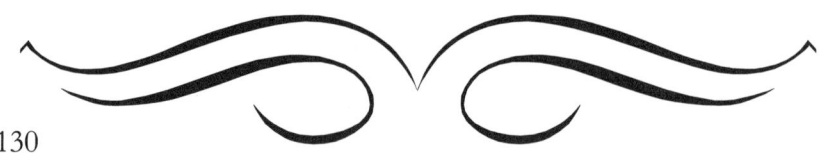

Chapter 11

Using
the Baqua

O nce we are able to determine the desire, what locations on
the Bagua support it and which ones balance it. To better
understand your path, you need to take a close look at what your
home is trying to tell you about your life. The Bagua is a tool that
helps you identify, raise and change the chi energy in your home.

Property

The first step in applying the Bagua is on the property itself.
This will add dimension and strengthen the foundation from which
to build other layers of the bagua. When laying the Bagua over the
plot of land it becomes clearer which areas need to be reinforced.
Areas that are missing can cause the chi to get lost or confused.

since many lots are not rectangular, it is common for areas to need strengthened.

Begin by drawing out the shape of your lot.

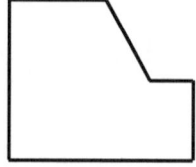

DRAW THE SHAPE OF YOUR PLOT OF LAND

You do not need to draw plot shapes to scale unless you are considering buying adjacent property or selling some of your attached acreage. If you currently have a house or buildings on the property ignore them for now. Look at the land as if it were a vacant lot. Make notes of the property front, tree line, power lines, roads, ponds, neighboring homes or anything that is closer than five feet to your property.

Next draw out the Bagua and label the sections with the Qualities of Life. (Refer to chapter 9)

Wealth	Fame	Love
Health	Yin/Yang	Children
Knowledge	Career	Helpful People

NEXT DRAW OUT THE BAGUA AND LABEL THE SECTIONS

Now superimpose the Bagua over the plot and inspect the results. Notice this lot is missing the entire love gua, which could suggest trouble with marriage or getting along with people in general. A slight section of the fame area is gone which could interfere with holding any political office or receiving recognition you deserve for your. Now if your dream was to be president of the P.T.A or a strong loving relationship, a strong foundation would not be present in this property without adjustments being made. We will discuss those later in this chapter.

Wealth	Fame	Love
Health	Yin/Yang	Children
Knowledge	Career	Helpful People

SUPERIMPOSE THE BAGUA OVER THE PLOT

When the plot of land that a home sits on has many acres, it is wise to sometimes divide the land into an inner yard and the outer yard. Especially land that is not used on a daily basis, many acres, large plots, farmland and wooded lots where not all the property is accessible.

Zesty Zetta

Zetta lived on twenty-five acres of woods. Only about five acres had been maintained and used as yard, the outer yard was used as a wind barrier and wildlife sanctuary. In this case she laid the Bagua on the perimeter of the property (outer yard) checking to see that all guas were in tact. When they weren't adjustments were made to square off the property. Then she laid a second Bagua on the inner property, the five acres surrounding her home. In the inner yard is her lawn, flowers, gardens, a pond and all the places that she and her family use as an extension of home.

Caution: When dividing property into parts, never lay out the Bagua on more than two layers without consulting a professional.

House applications

Now we can find where the qualities are located within the house itself. The Bagua is overlaid onto the shape of your home. The main entrance becomes the front of the property, providing that there is access to the door. Even if the front is seldom ever used and the home's occupants use another door or the garage, the front is still the front.

However, waterfront property or areas that are not easily accessible from the drive must use the driveway or street entrance as the front. Also, be sure to include anything that is attached to the home; garage, sunroom, porch and large decks.

The most desired shape is a rectangle, it represents all aspects of life are equal and intact. In homes where there are missing areas, it is not uncommon for people never to feel quite at home. There is almost always a feeling of uneasiness, nervousness or feeling out of "sorts".

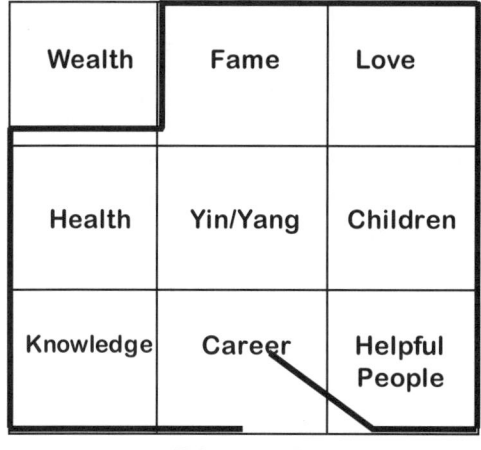

Wealth	Fame	Love
Health	Yin/Yang	Children
Knowledge	Career	Helpful People

Diagram B

If a home is irregular or missing a corner, it could imply an imbalance in the chi energy. For example if the wealth area is partially missing from your room (Diagram B), you could have problems holding onto money or making good investment decisions. When this occurs, strengthen each wall adjacent to the missing areas. Use artwork that is expensive, that depicts royalty, perhaps given to you by a wealthy relative, or art symbolic of wealth, riches, abundance or opportunity.

Wealth	Fame	Love
Health	Yin/Yang	Children
Knowledge	Career	Helpful People

Diagram C

135

Laying the Bagua over the entire house itself will shed some light on life situations that are going on now and those that have happened in the past. In diagram C, the occupants of this home may have problems with career or help when they need it.

When you lay the bagua on more than one level the bagua is the same on all levels. This includes; main floor, second floor, subsequent floors, lower levels, basements and attics.

Drawing Room Plans

The thought of drawing out room plans intimidates many people. This is the point where most folks become overwhelmed and not sure of how to do this important step. You do not have to be a great artist to draw out a floor plan. A simple sketch of an aerial view will do just fine. Don't make it fancy; squares, lines, rectangles and circles work well to denote all types of furnishings. This process of drawing out your home is the action needed to begin your journey of using Feng Shui - your Feng Shui.

**Start by drawing out one room
in your house.**

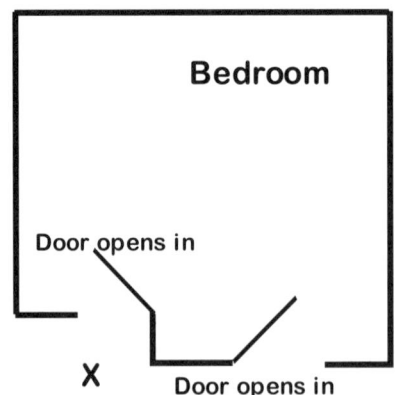

136

First, stand inside the door of the room and draw the basic shape of the outline. Then, add walls and closets. In some spaces, especially one-floor apartments, the living area can be one big room. When there are no walls dividing a space, split the area into designated sections such as sleeping area, dining area, etc., and work with each section as if it were an individual room.

Second, label the room, and notice anything that might be important. Missing areas, places that jut out into the room, closets, sliding doors leading outside, or sloped ceilings. Any architectural or structural feature that causes the room not to be square or rectangular should be noted. Label these with an X.

The mouth of the room

Thirdly pay attention to the door that leads into the room. Mark which way the door swings. Indicate this on your drawing.

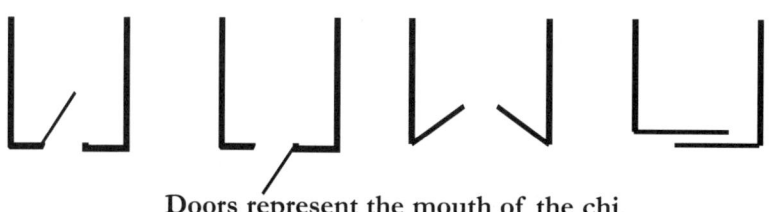

Doors represent the mouth of the chi.

It is important that you recognize the style of door you have for the room: Does it open inward, is it a single or a double door, does it slide, or open outward? Some rooms don't have doors; just openings. Actually, this is the best style of door, because there is no interference with the pattern of chi entering the room.

Since the chi enters by the door, it is imperative that the doors open freely and with no blockage. Make additional notes if the door hits another door, sticks, doesn't shut all the way — anything that prevents it from swinging open and closing freely. Every measure should be taken to allow the chi to move in a natural pattern.

Eyes of the room

Windows are the Feng Shui eyes of your home. They invite the nourishing influences of sunlight and air into our spaces. Pay close attention to the shape of your windows. Make sure to keep all windows in good condition, and replace cracked panes.

People become very aloof when living with small windows. The world through large windows is very different from that of a porthole. The entire world takes on a new perspective. More isn't necessarily better; too many windows weaken the chi, causing arguing between children.

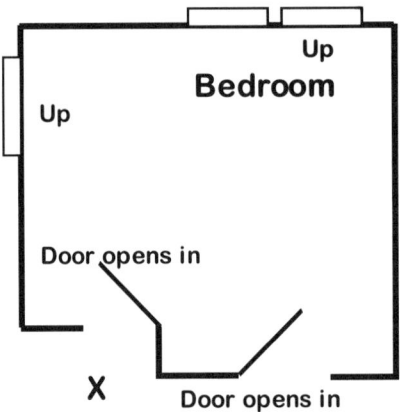

Windows represent the eyes of the chi

Windows that are exceptionally large or that have a wonderful view should be treated like picture frames. Painting them a different color than the walls will draw the eye to the beautiful picture of perfect scenery — not just an extra large window.

Windows round at the top that are arched or circular, give off a soothing; peaceful chi. Smooth shapes are considered relaxing, creative and inspiring. They enhance hallways, bedrooms and family rooms. Square and rectangular windows flatter eating areas; the kitchen and dining rooms. Skylights are glorious sources of light and energy. They invite the heavens into your home, while illuminating your peace of mind. They work best in cooking areas (not over the stove), small hallways, and foyers. Avoid sky-lights over the bed, because sleep will be erratic and unsettled.

The ideal Feng Shui window opens outward, symbolic of opening your arms and inviting the chi in for a big hug. Using a combination of different style windows is the most desirable.

Last but not least

Finally, using squares, circles, and lines, draw symbols to represent the furnishings in the room. Be sure areas that seem to collect newspapers, stuff and general clutter are clearly indicated with a question mark. Take one more look around your room, did you include everything? Is there a heater vent in the floor? Are you next to a business or parking lot?

Congratulations! You have completed a floor plan of your room. Now go around your home doing the same thing for each room. Take your time, drawing each room on a separate sheet of paper. Don't forget to do laundry rooms, halls, stairwells, and basements. Make notes as you go about anything you love and even those you don't.

Roomy Bagua

Now, determine what you desire, you need to determine what location on the Bagua supports it, and which one balances it. To better understand your path, you need to take a close look at what your home is trying to tell you about your life.

The Bagua is a tool that helps you identify, raise, and change the chi energy in your home.

After laying out the Bagua, look at the areas with a question mark. These areas that attract chaos, like laundry, clothes, books, and papers, can shed light on what is happening in your life. Let's say that you want to have a baby, but the chair where you always throw your clothes sits in that area.

Unfortunately the chi would have no way to circulate freely around that area of children because it is already full! Clear the pathway for the chi by removing any question marks you can. Once the path is open, miracles happen.

TheMystery of the missing Knowledge and Spirtuality Area.

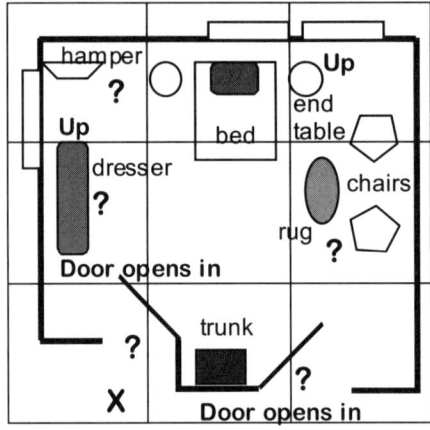

Caution: Consider **ALL** rooms in your space. Never ignore a room just because it isn't used often or is used for storage. All areas count when balancing chi, just as all areas count when balancing our lives.

Laying the Bagua over a room alerts you to which areas need to be strengthened. Areas that are missing can cause the chi to get lost or confused. Most homes are not rectangular; usually they will be missing sections of the Bagua.

In the diagram on the preceding page the room appears to be missing knowledge and spirituality (marked by the X.) However, since the closet is recessed the room isn't really missing any areas at all, but closets are challenging when trying to add symbols that represent intention. If working on knowledge and spirituality was the intention in this room, you should strengthen the outside of the closet as well as the inside. To accomplish this; organize the inside of the closet, discarding any unused clothing and hang picture of angels, or other spiritual artwork on the outside of the closet door.

Steps for Effectively Reading Rooms

1. Draw the outline of the room. Give it a name (My bedroom, Stella's room etc.)
2. Make a note of any missing area. (X)
3. Add doors, the size and the direction they open.
4. Add windows and the direction they open..
5. Indicates the location of main furnishings.
6. Mark with a (?) question mark areas that seem to gather chaos or clutter.
7. Lay the Bagua on the room.

Exercise:
Draw a floor plan of the room you are currently in. Label it with all the Qualities of Life. What quality are you sitting in ?

Program Students please complete the Using the Bagua Work sheet Number 1311

Wisdoms

Sun Rooms

Purpose:

Connecting to nature and the outdoors is the intention of this room. The symbolism of absorbing the sun daily rejuvenates us, keeping our personal chi abundant and radiant.

Suggestions:

Sunrooms are just that—sunny rooms make them beautiful. Use functional, sturdy furniture and keep all breakables out of the area. Create a peaceful haven to relax in.

Symbols:

Lush foliage and plants in sunroom invite the chi of confidence. Add floral print fabrics to chairs and keeping artwork breezy will encourage a steady flow of energy.

Color:

Pastels and light "summer" colors are best; use peach, yellow, blue and green. Where plants are abundant using white will enhance the leaf greens. Avoid using too much red

Adjusting
The Bagua

The Bagua is flexible it adapts to all size spaces. It can be used on a plot of land, a house or each room. Stretch it to include an entire complex or city or shrunk down and applied to the top of a desk. This Feng Shui tool will empower you to find potential problems and correct them *before* they appear as a real situation in your life.

Since not all lots are square, all homes rectangular, or rooms perfect; there comes a time when it is necessary to square off a space.

Wealth	Fame	Love
Health	Yin/Yang	Children
Knowledge	Career	Helpful People

143

**The rectangle in Feng Shui symbolizes Mother earth,
the heart of our life existence.**

Since chi travels effortlessly across Mother earth, the importance of reflecting her in your rooms is the goal. This begins with mimicking her rectangular shape.

As you create this rectangular shape you not only support the Quality of Life that is housed there but also adjust the overall wholeness of yourself.

These basic tools may used inside or outside to balance a space, improve the circulation of chi and to enhance one of the Qualities of Life.

Tools

1. Mirrors
2. Lights
3. Reflective objects
4. Sound
5. Life Forces
6. Heavy objects
7. Water features

8. Power objects
9. Color
10. Art
11. Movement
12. Personal Attributes
13. The elements
14. Attributes of the Quality of Life

Getting Into Shape

Check certain areas in your home to see if they live up to your aspirations and dreams or do they need to be reworked to support your journey. In this sections we will look at various missing areas in a home.

**Take what you can from this information and apply it
practically to your space.**

When missing areas need support, use more than one tool to add balance. For example, if you are missing the Wealth sector, be sure to stabilize the area with earth, symbolize big money with a personal symbol and then promote growth with the wood element.

Shape has major influence over our lives. The shapes that surround you have a great impact over how the chi energy will respond or not respond to your intention. Since we are striving to make all spaces rectangular, we need to take a look at shapes that can cause the chi to be blocked, low, stale or stagnate. Many homes have missing areas. Let's examine a few different shapes and ways to correct them.

The L Shape

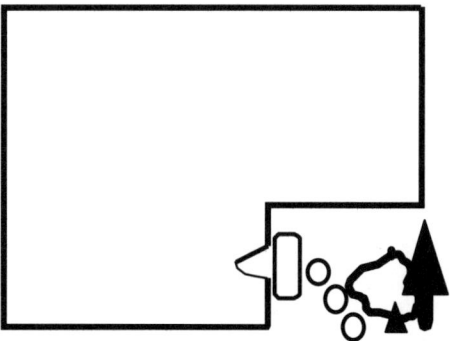

Square off this house with a grouping of trees and stepping-stones leading to the sidewalk. This will symbolically give a rectangular shape to the home. Helpful People is missing from this area. The circular stepping-stones laid out in a curvy pattern are attributes of Helpful People and Travel.

Below is the same shape in a bedroom. In cases like this, the remedies must be used inside the room. Use reflective surfaces like shiny picture frames to open up the area, a mat on the floor to stabilize the chi and a crystal-ceiling fixture to disperse the chi throughout the room.

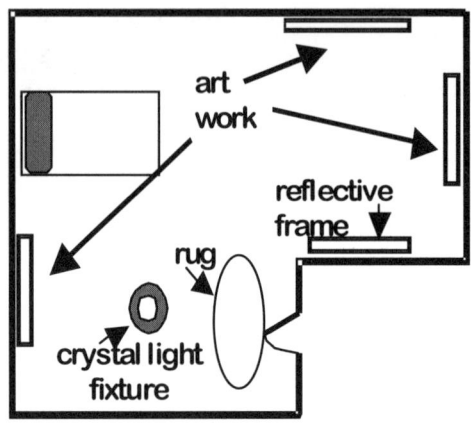

Add artwork with a path or road to invite the chi to "walk" on in. A serene painting of the woods would be a perfect symbol for Knowledge and Spirituality since this is the quality that is missing from the structure. This will symbolically give a rectangular shape to the room.

The U Shape

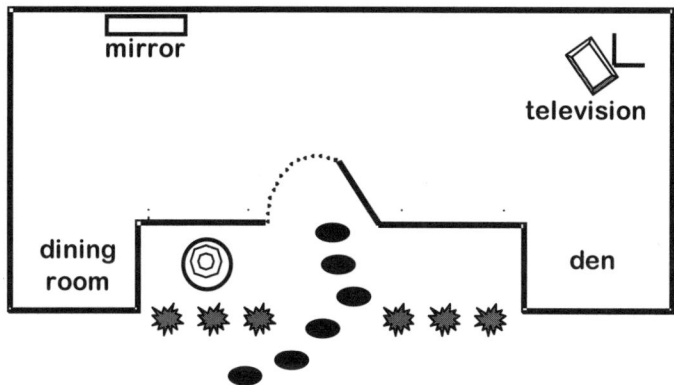

This U shape home takes on a square feeling with the use of bushes, fountains and a walk to the door. Since we are trying to strengthen the quality of Career, the fountain by the front door denotes flow and further supports Career.

Once inside, the mirror draws chi towards the dining room and electronic equipment pulls the chi towards the den. Which are both behind the chi entrance

Now let's look at the U shape inside the home. This is a fairly typical western bedroom. Many times we are unaware that a room is U shaped, but rooms with recessed closets often are.

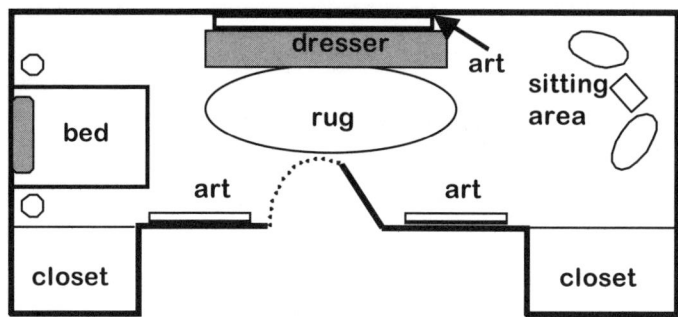

In this room we replaced the mirror over the dresser with art that is warm and inviting. An area rug directs the chi to the right and left. The seating area faces the door, thus welcoming the chi.

Artwork on either side of the door will expand the area, as will hanging a floral spray above the door. The wall that the door is on could also be painted a different color than the rest of the room to give the impression that the wall is being pushed back.

Since this room is missing Career, the art on either side of the door could depict pictures of the sea, a day at the beach or a beautiful pond.

Irregular Shape

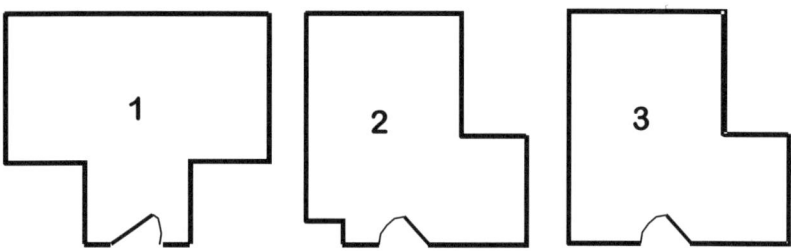

Irregular shapes happen for many reasons. Maybe a home was actually designed with a missing area to act as a private seating space. An architectural feature like a recessed fireplace will naturally cause walls to be pushed back, or simply the duct work from your furnace can cause a projection in a room.

Not all irregular shapes are bad Feng Shui.

An area that protrudes and is used as a quiet space to meditate and read leaves behind chi energy that is contemplative and nourishing. Fireplaces really do warm the soul by allowing the chi to be fervent and inviting. Turn unsightly projections into quaint nooks.

With your creativity and Feng Shui, you can turn any space into an artful balance of beauty and health.

Whenever a remedy is needed to square off your property, remember that the more tools you use, the better the reinforcement. Universal chi is attracted to symbols, and needs only a depiction to continue to move in the strongest pattern. This steady flow of vibrant chi keeps the pathways moving gracefully through our lives.

By clearly defining your intention, combining it with the Quality of Life that supports it, and then strengthening it using attributes and personal symbols; you create a powerful chi magnet. This brings an abundance of joy and opportunity right to your door by shaping not just your home, but also your life through Feng Shui.

The Feng Shui Workout

Every missing area has a remedy. This is a Feng Shui principle that can be followed to motivate the chi in a positive direction. These items differ depending on the Quality of Life and the personal symbol that is used.

Does the lower left sector of the house provide a place for you to read or study? Perhaps the knowledge and spirituality area is untidy, or belongs to someone else and you have no control over it. While the Knowledge and Spirituality area is about stillness, too much stillness will drain the action from the marriage area. Don't concentrate on one sector while paying little attention to complementary areas. Balance is crucial.

Here is a list of a few things that can be done with missing areas inside and outside the home. These are only samples; there are many other combinations to choose from.

If you are missing the Career Quality of Life

Outside:

Use a water feature outside and a black welcome mat by the front door.

149

Inside:

Install black flooring inside the front entrance. Add a picture of a waterfall.

If you are missing the Helpful People Quality of Life

Outside:

Use statuary in the garden of a helpful being like a fairy or a bird.

Inside:

Hang a travel poster or an item you bought while traveling.

If you are missing the Children Quality of Life

Outside:

Create a circular garden with white flowers, such as baby's breath, or add whimsical art.

Inside:

Use art made by children or hand made piece of art.

If you are missing the Love and Marriage Quality of Life

Outside:

Lay out plantings in pairs. Use statuary like love doves.

Inside:

In the missing area hang honeymoon pictures, a vase of roses or paint walls pink.

If you are missing the Fame and Reputation Quality of Life

Outside:

In the yard use a red garden globe or redwood furniture.

Inside:

Hang awards and affirmations of what your goal is.

If you are missing the Family and Health Quality of Life

Outside:

This is a great place for an herb garden or fruit bearing trees.

Inside:

Use healthy plants or stripe wallpaper. Green carpet and blue paint will support this area.

If you are missing the Knowledge and Spirituality Quality of Life

Outside:

Place a statue of an angel or Buddha in this area. Use Copper Verde yard ornaments.

Inside:

Place a bookshelf firmly against the wall; pull all the books to the front edge of the shelf.

If you are missing the Yin/Yang Quality of Life

Outside:

Rocks, stones, boulders, or items made from the earth such as concrete or statuary give earth stability.

Inside:

Use a globe, landscapes, or pictures of the earth or any item that represents making heaven here on earth.

Exercise:

Think about one of your dreams and which Quality of Life best supports it. Draw a floor plan of your bedroom, superimpose the Bagua over it. Now, look at the location of that Quality of Life in the room. Does it block or support your dream?

Program students please complete the Adjusting the Bagua Work sheet Number 1415

Wisdoms

Apartments and Condominiums

Purpose:

These small homes are a refugee to protect and nourish our soul. They are sanctuaries that keep the chi rich and fruitful. Though scaled down in square footage, there is nothing small about their charm.

Suggestions:

Embellishing the front door using a decorative mat, wreath or hanging a bell on the door all personalize the entrance. Just inside the door, hang decorative art that draws you inside.

Symbols:

Animal prints add mystery and protection. Celestial art simulates stability. Brass on the door acts like a chi "magnet" attracting the chi of opportunity.

Color:

If you must leave walls white then accent with green for health, reds for motivation, blue for serenity, purple for peace and yellow for balance.

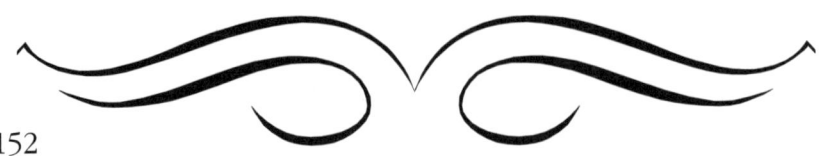

A Balancing Act

It was around my eighth birthday, and my sister decided to teach me how to ride a bicycle, which, by the way, was no easy feat. What began with one day would turn into a week long series of "crash and burn" attempts on my part to master the art. However, I was determined to learn, because those two wheels were a sense of freedom that my friends had and I lacked.

A freedom I WANTED!

I would pump the pedals and my sister would jog along side of me holding onto the rear of the bike to steady it. Naturally, the harder I tried, the faster I peddled which made it impossible for her to hang on. I would soar eight feet, lose my balance, and crash to the ground. If the bangs and scrapes weren't too bad, we'd try again. If they were, we'd wait until another day.

Eventually I mastered the task. I remember the day I glided out of my sister's hands and down the street on my own. Behind me I could hear her cheer. In front of me was the adventure of seeing and experiencing things on my own. By shifting my weight from side to side, I could balance myself. I soon discovered that not only could I keep from falling, I could make that bike fly. It was a fabulous feeling.

In those days I preferred climbing trees to playing with dolls. We had an old Banyan tree in our yard, and much to my mother's dismay, I would explore the highest branches. The best part was wiggling out on a branch, and while assuming a Tarzan stance; I would pronounce myself queen of the tree. Now this expert posture would consist of me standing flatfooted on the branch, beating on my chest and letting out a great howl, all the while balancing my weight so as to not topple backwards. I don't think my Mother exhaled the entire time I was between the ages of seven and twelve.

Natural Order

As children we learn many ways to keep our balance — riding bicycles, climbing trees, skating and surfing. Learning to keep our balance is an important step in being able to perform to our body's highest potential.

Through Feng Shui we are able to keep that natural order by reflecting the balance within us, in our homes, and the spaces where we spend time. This will allow our personal chi to reach its fullest potential, which reflects back into our lives.

Creating situations in our surroundings that nourish us and keep us completely balanced goes beyond the mere physical. It is a delicate array of mind, body and spirit.

Learning the art of Feng Shui includes many facets.

Understanding how the chi energy works, and obtaining the knowledge of how it directly affects us are two very important factors. However, there is a third factor that bridges the knowledge with the understanding of the universal law of energy. This is the conscious act of balancing, that which is not secure.

There are many things that we can use to begin to balance a space. Some items add beauty or a sense of peace while adding ambiance to a space. Certain situations feel unsettling and need to be secured, while others need help getting the chi energy to flow. The items that we use to accomplish this balance within our homes are called Feng Shui tools.

Though there are many tools, the key is to know how and when to use them. Using a tool incorrectly can lead to unsuccessful results or an imbalance in the energy. The first step is being able to determine what type of tools to use and then applying them properly in order to use the tools to their fullest potential. Having a big Feng Shui tool "box" is a great help when handling life's situations. We then become more than just the carpenters of our spaces; we become the curator of chi.

What are Tools?

We have discussed how the elements are tools that can be used with certain Qualities of Life. The elements have strengthening features that other tools don't have. However, other tools can be used alone or in conjunction with the elements to change or heighten the chi around a given situation. When items are used together with the element and the quality, a three-deep layer of positive action is present.

Tools are items that are used to strengthen areas that either need balancing or more action in a life situation.

> For example, let's say that you are looking for a soul mate. When you lay the Bagua on your floor plan, the love and marriage area is missing from your home. Then you would use a tool to add the missing area. If the love and marriage area is intact, that is part of the structure. You would then

want to get more energy moving towards supporting you in your search.

Though the tool you use could be the same to do both tasks, they would not necessarily be used in the same way. Some of the tools that are used are color, mirrors, lights, crystals, sound, living art, nature, water, wind, aroma, art, sheen, and personal items. When mixing any tool with an element, we strengthen the entire process of balance.

Tools move the chi towards a positive direction.

By using tools in conjunction with each other, you are creating the most effective cure possible. The combination of using the correct tool (body) to your intention (mind) with the application of the strongest chi (spirit) completes the triangle of the ultimate universal chi.

The Vital Color Role

There are colors we love, and those we don't. Color plays a vital role in our overall concept of the world. The flow of earth energies can be halted or ignited by color. The fact that the earth is not monochromatic only reinforces the need to have color around us. Colors symbolically represent a certain type of chi. Red can be described as warm and tingling; blue as cool and calm. When we look at this from a health standpoint, color is not just visual but vibrates at an energetic level.

Black, red and purple symbolize wealth and happiness.
Brown and tan bring focus and grounding properties.
Yellow and gold increase intellect and prosperity.
Green and blue are or growth and rebirth
Teal and aqua are for spiritual awareness and serenity.

Certain colors have symbolisms that identify the type of chi attracted to them. These colors have this attachment regardless where in the home they are used.

For example: Red is the most yang color and is linked with fire energy. The chi around fire is fast, igniting and exciting.

Red is associated with romance, wealth and notoriety. Use it in the love gua of your home to ignite the fire of passion, or in the career area as an agent to quicken your search for a job.

Yellow
Adds a sense of space; works great with natural sunlight.
Lifts mood, encourages flexibility and inspires optimism.
Stimulates joy, symbolically represents wisdom and intuitiveness.
Use in kitchens, and dining rooms.

Orange
Stimulates activity, sociability and enthusiasm.
Invites conversation; promotes learning and adventure.
Use in kitchens, living rooms, dining areas, offices and workstations.

Red
Romantic, passionate, motivating and strong.
Associated with courage, excitement, and assertiveness.
A powerful color; should be used in small quantities.
Use in kitchens, powder rooms, living rooms and family rooms.

Pink
A symbol of spiritual healing, gentleness, sweetness and innocence.
Youthful as in "tickle me pink"; a symbol of good health or as in description, as of rosy cheeks.
A sign of love, romance, good relations and feeling perky.
Use in powder rooms, bathrooms, children's rooms and bedrooms.

White

Purity, harmony, and balance.
Symbolizes truth; unbiased and religious rite.
Signifies the child, inner work or neutral side.
Use shades of white to change a room's chi or to soften any color.

Earth Tones

Sense of nurturing, nature and vitality.
Restful, peaceful and rejuvenating.
Adds balance and aids in stability and security.
Defines a space - warm, inviting, and sound.
Use in bedrooms, family rooms, home offices, reading rooms and dens.

Black

Associated with mystery and the unknown.
Absorbing, silent, dramatic, and powerful.
The abyss, inner depth, void, or classic style; associated with a graceful course.
Use in offices, living rooms, and kitchens.

Green

Crisp, healthy, sharp and refreshing.
Replenishing growth and energizing
Associated with new beginnings, spring and healing.
Use in bedrooms, baths, meditation rooms, healing rooms, and places of worship.

Blue

Soothing, sedated, quiet and calming.
Has antiseptic qualities and is said to reduce pain.
Balancing opens communication and creativity.
Use in bedrooms, baths, healing rooms, schools, and gyms.

Purples

Spirituality, hierarchy, and physic intuition.
Reduces hunger, decreases mental fatigue and supports abundance

Soothing, associated with good intentions calming and magical
Use in meditation areas, bedrooms, baths, saunas, and breakfast rooms.

Color is a tool that changes and influences the chi.

Wearing color

Color can has such a strong vibration that even the visually impaired claim that they can actually *feel* the difference between shades.

This powerful, and colorful chi attracts many positives. Wearing certain colors can make a statement by giving the Universe a clear message to support what you want to obtain.

PERSONAL COLOR GUIDE

	Selling Something	Job Hunting	Finding Love	Discovering Joy	Finding Spirituality	Adopting Good Health
Blue, Green, Aqua, Teal	Neutral	Yes	Neutral	Yes	Yes	Yes
Off White, White, Beige	Yes	No	Neutral	No	Yes	Neutral
Gray, Black, Navy, Eggplant	Neutral	Yes	No	Neutral	Yes	Neutral
Yellow, Tan, Orange, Peach, Brown	Neutral	Yes	Yes	No	No	Yes
Rose, Red, Pink, Peach, Blush	Yes	No	Yes	Yes	No	No

To attain a goal, use color as a good luck tool when trying to sell something, job-hunting, looking for joy, seeking spiritual guidance, to improve health and many other aspects. Use the Personal Color Guide to help you select the right color that will boost your energy level when you need to accomplish certain tasks.

Mirrors: the True Image

Mirrors are not only a tool, but are also symbolic of the water element. Convex mirrors expand areas, opening up a space by giving it a wider view. This works great for drawing in a pretty view to an otherwise dismal area, making hallways and aisles appear wider and expanding the width of rooms. Concave mirrors turn large oppressive images into round intimate pictures. By taking the central focus off of them they seem to almost disappear. Using a concave mirror diminishes the reflection of a large item, like a tree, that cast a foreboding shadow over a door or entrance.

Large mirrors draw in positive images and opens up a space, where small mirrors deflect negative energy away from a space. Mirrors stimulate by adding dimension and duplicate positives by doubling images through its reflection by adding life to a room.

Lighten Up

Lights set a mood whether it is quiet or exciting. Diffused light is quiet and peaceful; bright light is stimulating and active. Use lighting to soften dark corners and to soothe the energy. Uplift the chi by using lights low to the ground and angling them upward.

To add solidity to an area that is missing, create a wall of light from spotlights angled downward. To arouse and illuminate the chi in a low energy area, dim lights work better than bright lights. Bright light stimulates work that needs to be done quickly. All lighting is related to the fire element. This includes anything that gives off light including lamps, candles, bulbs, fireplaces and sunshine.

Shimmer and Shine

We are creatures that love baubles, especially ones that shine. Regardless what the item is made of, we are attracted to the shimmer and glow. These items brighten, expand and lift chi. Getting the chi moving in a natural pattern is what they do best. Adding, "zing" to an otherwise dreary area is their job. Some examples of things that shine are: crystal prisms, brass, coins, reflective surfaces, silks, sequins, and cut glass.

Sound Makers

It is easy for the chi to get stuck or low. Sound keeps the chi circulating. To instantly change the feeling in a room, add a beautiful sound; the room will come alive with that sound. Sound makers include: wind chimes, instruments, music, stereos, singing and chirping birds, and pendulums on clocks and bells. To prove the power of sound, play a radio outside and watch the squirrels, chipmunks and birds as they are drawn to the sound.

Living Art and Objects of Nature

In their natural state these items have a strong earth energy attached to them. When used in the home, this energy is dispersed throughout the home leaving grounding and stability behind. Nature has a very nurturing essence attached to it, which soothes unsettled feelings. Examples of these objects are: plants, pets, bird nests, flowers, humans, leaves, and shells.

Heavy Objects

Weight is a great way to steady the energies. Where light uplifts, weight stabilizes giving an area a sense of well-being and security. Think of a wobbly chair and a concrete bench. Heavy objects leave a sense of security that gives a good foundation to the situation that it depicts.

Examples: statues, stones, concrete items, large pieces of furniture and other hard to move objects.

Water Features

Very important elements, as well as a masterful tool are water features. Water purifies, flows, nourishes, diminishes and cleanses the chi in the home, workplace, yard and even community.

Even the smallest amount of moving water can bring an abundance of opportunity in your home. Examples: aquariums, fountains, birdbaths, bowls, snow globes, ponds and streams.

Wind Dancers

Movement cause the chi to change direction, it disperses negative chi and circulates positive chi. Calling the energy to a particular location is its main function. Use items such as mobiles, windsocks, whirligigs, flags, kites, ropes, weather vanes, streamers, and tassels.

Works of Art

Art has many attributes and can be used in many ways. Paintings with paths can make you feel as if you want to walk into them. This will draw positive chi and is great for foyers or entries. Pictures of vacations can hold wonderful memories, where statues can add grace and weight to an unsupported area.

The Chinese have a saying, "Everything is always talking to you, make sure it has nice things to say".

Take time to add just the right art in your home, its best use is to constantly remind you of your dreams and point you in that direction. Find art symbols that move you forward.

Powerful Electrical Objects

To convey strength and force is important when you need to support an area, maintain a life-style, or hold up to a situation. Electrical object hold the charge of natural energy, and an enormous amount of chi. Examples: computers, TV sets, neon lights, automobiles, and electrical appliances.

Aromas and Scents

The sense of smell is a powerful tool. Not just a Feng Shui adjustment, certain essential oils actually change the vibration of the energy in a space. Essential oils have properties that make them powerful tools for working with the energy fields of both our bodies and our environment. Scent can take you into the future by setting up a framework in which to move. It can purify, stimulate, soothe and heal both the body and the home. Aromas are considered one of the good luck tools since they are so powerful. The methods of using scent as a power instrument are endless. Some ways to use them are: candles, bath salts, soap, incense, diffusers, potpourri, simmering pots, and incense.

Personal Items

Personal items expand, enliven and strengthen. They give us a sense of who we are; the meaning should be very profound to the owner. Heirlooms and antiques give us history and is the very foundation of our person. This tool is the ultimate chi enhancement when we love the item and it holds deep meaning for us. Personal items are private, intimate objects that hold the affection of *your* heart. Use these in conjunction with any other tools or alone when drawing positive chi towards a private matter.

Manual Effort

Using physical activity to complete a goal allows the energy to change. Rearranging furniture, removing clutter, adding symbols, or shifting obstacles all take manual effort to accomplish. Kinetic energy is the amount of force needed to change or move an object and this task of moving items opens pathways for natural chi patterns. This pattern changes the direction of the chi, drawing it to an otherwise restricted area.

The Elements

Water element - effortless, upward flow
Metal element - detailed, sharp, creative
Fire element - action, social, exciting
Wood element - growth, new, nurturing
Earth element - strong, steady, powerful

When tools are used in conjunction with an element, the chi is raised to a higher level without any action from us. An example of this would be framing a painting that you did (personal symbol) with a gold frame (metal element) and hanging it in the Children and Creativity (see Bagua) area of your home. Each element represents the chi that is attached to it. Using the element as a power tool gives a clear message of intention.

Exercise:

What colors do you like? Which are your least favorite? What color could strengthen your dreams and desires? Which one will diminishes the obstacle standing in the way of your dream?

Program students please complete A Balancing Act Work sheet Number 1413

wind

water

Wisdoms

Sacred Place

Purpose:

A sacred space that joins body, mind, and spirit. This is where we go to be one with the universal energy. The place to connect to our higher source; an asylum to express our rare inner beauty.

Suggestions:

The emphasis is on how the space feels not looks. A quite serene setting, — a space that "whispers". Allowing contemplation on the single most important ingredient, you.

Symbols:

A sparse environment denotes room to mature and develop. Art work and statuary of spiritual figures you admire strengthen conviction. Inspirational sounds such as bells, wind chimes, a bubbling fountain or music inspires commitment and promise.

Color:

Teal, aqua and turquoise are the colors of choice. Shades in the purple family support intuition; where using black sparingly increases the inner depth of the soul.

Chapter 14
Confirming Your Purpose

Finding a place to be alone with our thoughts is the reason Feng Shui is sought after in the first place. One good reason for using Feng Shui is to find ways that are safe and comfortable to live and work. This allows us to feel an inner tranquility at all times. Ideally a sacred place should be that part of us, deep inside where you find peace and serenity — that connection to your true self.

Sacred places can mean many things. Perhaps it's a church, a mountain, a still pool or a walk in the woods. It is a place where we feel the universal energies, oneness with spirit, a connection to a deity or the presence of something very special. That isn't always easy with all the events, good and unpleasant, that surrounded us while growing up and shaping our lives.

The very things we want around us can actually taint the way we feel about our homes. We know that our life is a mirror image of our circumstances. What Feng Shui gives us are the tools to reflect back into us all the positives that the world has to offer. We do this by beginning to create a sacred, special place where we live and work today. When we do this, they reflect the true us; the way we have always wanted to be.

Our Home, Our Work

The first step in creating a special place, a haven, is to make your space your own, here and now — today! Even if where you are living is temporary, claim the space as yours. Everyone is a unique individual; so is our life. To clarify that uniqueness is to contemplate on how to use the space you are in for your greatest good.

One great way to do that is by naming your house, respecting the deity of chi energy that resides there. I have heard many different names for homes: Jessica, Frangelica, Goldie, Chenille, Hasta, La Casa, and even Bob. It isn't what you call your home that matters, but that you give her or him a personality. Many of my clients swear that once they named their house it became easier to decorate. It was like when they shopped, they could pick things out and know instantly whether it would work in the space or not. "Oh, that fabric is something Jessica (the house) would love!" Have you ever gone shopping and saw a sweater and knew instantly that your sister would love it? Shopping for your house takes on a new meaning when you shop for La Casa or Bob; not to mention it is a lot more fun.

Another way to claim the space is by a physical action that imbeds the intention deep into the walls. Painting, hanging pictures, refinishing furniture, adding a throw pillow, an area rug, rearranging the furniture, bringing in plants, installing window treatments, wallpapering, and adding things you love, all make the connection between the physical act and spiritual transformation making this collection of rooms into a safe haven in which to thrive.

Clearing the space

At times the spaces where we live and work don't feel "right" to us. Though you have cut down on the clutter, claimed the space as yours, and followed good Feng Shui practices; often it can feel like something is still missing. Even when items may be discarded, the residual energy that was attached to them sometimes still lingers. Clearing away the stagnant energy from your space will lift the vibration of the chi in the home.

Tools used for clearing

Using *white sage and smudge sticks* is a great way to clear stuck energies. Smudge sticks come in many fragrances such as cedar, lavender, mint, etc. The fragrance should coincide with the overall intention for your quality of life. Light the edge of the smudge stick and begin by using the stick around the outside of your body to clear any stuck chi from around your person.

Carry it through each room, being careful to keep it over a dish to catch any falling ashes. The ashes symbolically represent change; as the sticks change to ash the space clears of stale chi.

While moving from room to room, repeat the above steps using affirmations of a positive intention.

Some examples of positive affirmations while you clear your spaces are:

We are a loving family that supports each other in all that we do.

Angelica, (or house name) binds all that is joy, love, and serenity in our family.

Use your own words to talk to the guardian of your home making them part of your family. Understand that it isn't the words that matter but your honest sincerity. Continue on with your smudge sticks allowing the smoke to flow over all furnishings, art and accessories; making certain the smoke bellows into the corners, the closets and every little niche. Smoke is a natural healer. To Native Americans the smoke is breath of the flame, and the flame ignites the living being of fire. When you have gone through all the rooms in your house with the smudge or sage, the entire space will take on a healthy glow much like the land does after it rains.

Sometimes when there has been a traumatic event, death, or ill fortune attached to a home; smudging alone may not work and a complete space clearing needs to be done. In those cases, there are many great books on space clearing at your local bookstore. After reading about other techniques if you still do not feel comfortable performing the task yourself, contact an expert in the art of space clearing.

My belief is this - A home should always whisper!

Creating an Altar

To have a complete sacred place, an important addition is an altar. An altar doesn't have to be spiritual in nature, just a place where you put special things you love. The main reason to have an altar is to have a place where you can go and focus, if only for a few minutes a day. It releases the stress of the day, or an event and draws all things positive to you and your family. Use it to meditate, pray, write or just sit. Create a ceremony when there, by lighting a candle, burning incense, ringing bells, singing or playing music.

My alter

In our home, the end of our hall is where the altar is. It is a wooden shelf hung on the wall and above it hangs a painting done by my husband. On it there is a candle given to me by my sister-in-law, a candle holder from my niece's wedding, a picture of my guardian angel, a plate from my mother, a photo of flowers from our garden and a small vase that was a gift from my daughter. These personal items have glorious memories attached to them. They make me feel good and evoke a deeper sense of happiness and home —a sense of knowing where I am and that I belong.

Whatever you use on your altar, it should make you smile and give you a warm, inviting feeling. When you feel good it draws an abundance of positive chi to the area around the altar and throughout the entire house, and touches the lives of all that live and visit your divine home.

Sanctuary: Finding Sacred Spaces

When we left home to finally be on our own, we thought we were grown - well, at least adult. Looking back at our youthful attempts at life situations makes us smile at our being so naive. It usually didn't take us long to find out we still had many lessons to learn.

It's been proven that we are products of our environment, that the way we've been brought up influences our lives. But if that is true, why as adults are we so different from other adults in our family? If we grew up in the same loving home, why don't we think, act and react the same? Because we continue to grow, develop and change daily throughout our lives. Each day we are given a chance to begin again, start fresh. The Universe is here to give us an abundance of chi energy to catapult us towards anything new we desire.

Live life to the fullest

I know elderly people that sit and let the loneliness of life destroy them. So, caught up in uncertainty as to what to do, they do nothing, and that nothingness kills the soul. Inaction stops the heart from beating. When we were children, the world seemed so big, and now most of us just see the world as our own piece of it.

The truth is the world is still big and quite frankly; I want a bigger piece of it than I have now. In these days of hearing how the world is on a downhill spiral, I strongly protest. This grandiose world is on an upward swing of amazement and wonder with a flourish of chi pushing from behind. Please walk with gently steps on her.

As you continue your studies, your knowledge will mature into a more profound philosophy; one that can be handed on to others that come after you.

Feng Shui has had such a marvelous impact on my life and I am so grateful for all that it has done and continues to do for me. My wish is that you too have found a wondrous passion and that your life will be forever changed.

Exercise:
Spend a few moments walking through your home, and with a light touch, run your fingers across the walls. While sitting quietly, spend some time naming your house. Involve your entire family and once a week, light a candle and thank the Diva of your home and the Universe for the rich abundant life you have.

Program students please complete the Confirming Your Purpose Work sheet Number 1414

Personal Tutor

How The Programs Works

The Feng Shui - A Course of Study Personal Tutor Program is designed to be gentle on you and your time. That's why you can complete the course in your time; not ours. Each book has several chapters that are divided into sections. The length of a chapter depends on how extensive the content. In other words, a chapter may be divided into one to four sections. Chapters are broken up to make the level of understanding easier. This course is not graded; it is only evaluated on your level of understanding.

At the end of a section or chapter, you will be asked to complete an exercise and a work sheet. Once you register for the **Personal Tutor Program**, new extensive work sheets with clear visuals will be sent to you. When you have completed the assignments for each chapter, return them to your tutor. They will be personally evaluated and sent back to you.

Your Personal Tutor Program Includes:

- Private Student Identification
- Evaluation of all your work
- Your own Personal Tutor
- Help when you need it
- Forty - five minutes personal time with your Tutor
- Privileged access to the *Feng Shui Internet Forum*
- Priority Status

If you have a question about a particular section of the workbook or one of your assignments, you are always welcome to call or e-mail your Personal Tutor. To insure that your questions are answered, a second tutor is assigned to you in the case the first one is unavailable when you call.

Besides personal evaluations, your tutor is here to answer _your_ questions. If you need clarity on an assignment or if you have a question about your own home, your tutor is there to help.

But it doesn't stop there. We know that sometimes you will need the chance to spend several uninterrupted and focused minutes with a Feng Shui professional. So you will also receive three, fifteen minute one - on - one sessions to talk about anything you choose.

In addition, as a student of the Feng Shui Course of Study Personal Tutor Program, you have privileged access to our _Feng Shui Internet Forum_ where you can participate in an open online discussion with Feng Shui experts and other students. To top off our program, you will also receive priority status, which gives you first choice at any of our hands-on classes.

To reward you for all your hard work, students who participate in our Feng Shui Tutor Program will receive a beautiful:

Certificate of Completion

Upon finishing all the assignments in each book completed, in _The Feng Shui Course of Study Personal Tutor Program_. Proof that you have received the most in-depth information available for any in-home personal development study program.

To register for your Personal Feng Shui Tutor or to ask more about this program call: 1-888-882-2261 or write:

Ohio Design Inc. and Quality Life Workshops
Email: www.ohiodesigninc.com

Contact Information

Ohio Design and Quality Life Workshops is one of the largest groups of Feng Shui Professionals in the country. EM "Penny" Crabtree and her gifted professionals are available for presentations, workshops and to provide Feng Shui evaluations for home and business. Contact them at: 1-888-882-2261 For information regarding our Professional Consultant training program, to become a Feng Shui tutor or a Course Facilitator contact:

Ohio Design, Ltd.,
3594 Stockholm Rd., Suite 1A
Columbus, OH 43081- 4242
(614) 523-2872

To obtain your Personal Feng Shui Tutor, book a speaker or request a copy of our current class schedule please call:
1-888-882-2261

For information on our other Feng Shui books, tapes and videos or to request a catalog, please call the above number or:

Visit our web site:
www.ohiodesigninc.com
www.theleftside.com

Or e-mail us at:
Ohiodesigninc@aol.com

Quality Life Workshops™
Presents
The Ultimate Course

Feng Shui -
Professional Program
& Bonus Workshops

Correcting Challenges
Advanced Floor Plans
Commercial Principles
Witness an Actual Feng Shui Consultation
Be Part of a Live Feng Shui Presentation
Receive a one on one consultation session

Bonus Workshops

Feng Shui & the Garden: Use color and design outdoors
My Brief Case: Preparing for a Feng Shui consultation
Empowering Success ™ - A unique marketing Program.
Consultant Techniques ™ - Performing the most effective consultations.

Included with this program:

Facilitator Training: become a teacher of
The Feng Shui Course of Study
Feng Shui - Professional Extended Program

For information
***Call* 1-888-882-2261**